iEmployment

A Voter Guide to Economic Recovery

Charles Cantoni

iEmployment

Copyright © 2013 by Charles Cantoni

Second Edition

ISBN-13: 978-1479305872
ISBN-10:   1479305871

Printed in USA by CreateSpace

Dedication

This book is dedicated to those who find it difficult if not overwhelming to find employment during the extended after-effects of the Great Recession, i.e. those who "Can't find work when the economy stinks."

iEmployment

Contents

Preface

The economic setback in the U.S. (the Great Recession) that occurred in the 2008-2009 timeframe has led to a serious lack of jobs. It has resulted in unemployment rates of around 8% four years later. Even worse, it has led to under-employment rates of around 15% or higher. Debate over the best approach to be taken to cure the problem is rampant. "iEmployment" is my view of what needs to be done to recover from the high underemployment rates.

I've written this book from the viewpoint of a concerned individual (about unemployment in the U.S.) that has had many work experiences in life, including raising money for ventures and being President and CEO of several medical instrumentation companies. I've worked in the fields harvesting fruit, as an unskilled laborer, as a forklift driver, as a skilled electrician and welder, as a sheet metal apprentice, as a Lieutenant in the United States Army, as a design engineer, as an engineering manager, and as president and CEO of four medical imaging companies. I've raise money for startups as an employee shareholder, as a limited partner investor, as a founder of medical imaging companies, from venture capitalists, and as founder of a Sub-chapter S Corporation.

In September 2011 I took part in an immersion travel seminar to Nicaragua to better understand the poverty situation in that county, Nicaragua being one of the poorest countries in the Western Hemisphere. While the country has an unemployment rate of about 8% it is clear that Nicaragua has a really severe underemployment problem; more like 55% of the people live on incomes of less than $2.50 per day. The problem, then, is to figure out how best to create jobs.

You may be wondering, "Why bring up Nicaragua if we are talking about the U.S. economy?" Well, Nicaragua has a population of around 6 million people and an area about the size of New York State. One can readily examine the natural resources, imports, exports, and the job situation. It is an impoverished society, and it therefore serves as a "thought model" that helps one develop a plan of attack to combat poverty in general. You'll notice in this book that I revert to Nicaragua occasionally in presenting illustrations of potential economic problems. I do this because the country represents such a stark contrast as compared to wealthier countries. The illustrations are thus easier to quantify.

Thinking through the problem, I became convinced that we in the United States, as a country, really do know how to create jobs in a free market capitalistic environment. We have years and years of experience with successes and setbacks (guided by theory, learning in the school of hard knocks). In working on possible solutions to the Nicaragua problem, as severe as it is, it became clear that one needs to think through the economic development process from a fundamental viewpoint.

In short, one needs to examine many points of view and the many factors that go into economic development in a society. Such analysis includes consideration of the nature of free market capitalism and the goals of social justice – they at times appear to be in conflict.

iEmployment thus reflects my thoughts on the economic development of a society wherein unemployment is a critical issue. It is clearly a critical issue in Nicaragua, and I will argue that it is a critical issue in parts of the U.S. and, obviously, in many other countries of the world. Our focus at present is on the United States, but the problems causing unemployment are common in many societies. As stated, it is a complex problem to solve, requiring the understanding of many different aspects of economic development.

My hope is that by reading this book, you will develop and/or improve your understanding of the under-employment problem and suggested solutions. In the United States, government action and/or inaction can fundamentally influence the probability of success. Perhaps this book will give you ideas on how to evaluate those running for office, perhaps serve as a kind of "Voter Guide to Economic Recovery."

Finally, I'm going to explore in this book your roll as a voter that goes beyond politics. I'm talking about actions that you, as a citizen, can take that will greatly enhance the process. Ah, personal responsibility is a wonderful burden on us all. But then again, wouldn't you prefer lower taxes that typically come with economic growth?

1...Introduction

Historical Perspective

Midway through 2013, we in the United States find ourselves in a continuing economic slowdown (that has resulted from the Great Recession). The slowdown initially met the requirements of being called a true recession. While the recession is technically over, the slowdown is not. Economic growth is hovering at a 2% annualized rate and underemployment is in the vicinity of 15% nationwide[1] and as high as 20% in California, Nevada and certain segments of our society.[2]

Our country has been through the technology stock bubble and then the housing market bubble and subsequent collapse, triggering the Great Recession. We end up with an unreasonably high percentage of people living below the poverty line. (The economic growth rate is important because we are trying to pull out of the recession – we need

---

[1] That's about 23 million people out of the total estimated employable workforce of 155 million people in the United States

[2] In a Wall Street Journal Opinion piece published on September 7. 2012 Mortimer Zuckerman wrote that there are an additional 8 million people that have given up looking for work. Including these folks, the real overall unemployment rate is closer to 19%.

high growth numbers in order to achieve improved employment.)

How we arrived at this situation is the subject of much debate. From the very general viewpoint, the people in government have had problems in setting into place policies and laws that provide for a smoothly functioning economy. In the technology stock bubble, for example, we had a belief among many economists, and the Federal Reserve in particular, that huge multiples of price to earnings ratio on new technology stocks were the "new paradigm." Too many analysts and investors believed it, running up stocks to unreasonable levels, aided by low interest rates set by the Federal Reserve. This of course was then followed by a collapse. In the collapse, many average citizens were caught with significantly reduced value to their retirement accounts.

Then came the housing bubble. Many in government were anxious to see more home ownership. But instead of working on the fundamentals of how incomes might improve to allow more home ownership, the push was to lower the qualification standards for home mortgages. Thus sub-prime mortgages were being implemented. Sub-prime means here's your mortgage, even though we pretty well know that you cannot afford it. This drove demand to higher levels, causing prices to ramp up.

Some in the financial markets sensed the problem and bundled up mortgages, good and bad, to be resold as a package to investors. When the bubble finally burst, too many home owners were caught with mortgages that were above the home values (upside down) and the bundled mortgage packages containing a mix of normal and sub-prime mortgages were a disaster. Banking institutions were caught up in the downturn, in some cases requiring loans from the Federal Government to bail them out.

We are still seeing the effects of the bubble bust with continuing decline in home values and continuing fore-closures, effects that have lasted at least into early 2013. I won't go into the myriad of details here on the bank rescue programs, etc. But safe to say, the economy took a big hit. In the ramp up, home building was on a roll. As a result, unemployment was very low and things were booming. When the bubble burst, a huge number[3] of construction folks were suddenly out of work.

When folks can't find work, they pucker up and stop spending money – spending only for essentials. That brings down the market for goods, and away we go into a recession. (An important point here: in our economy, the domestic demand for goods and services is an important element of our total markets, so in a sense, our economy is as good as the employment situation is good.) I'll talk more later on about the coupling between the health of our economy and the wages people earn.

I do not intend to play a blame game here; my goal is to write about how we can go about getting back on track economically (actually the goal is to be better than just "back on track"). But the point is, we have hit a few major bumps in the economic road, caused basically by a lot of people (in and out of government) making some bad judgments.

---

[3] Estimated by some to be in the vicinity of 8 million jobs lost. When you consider the impact of these 8 million leaving the marketplace except for bare necessities, the total impact of these losses feeds over into further job losses.

I've run a number of companies, and it's really simple when you go about doing your planning for success – you just <u>have to be right</u>. You dream, you analyze, you plan and you execute. If you're right, yahoo! If you're wrong, yikes, better go back to the drawing board and adjust the plan! When you are in the national government, and especially when you are a part of the Federal Reserve System and you're wrong, your fanny is exposed big time, and we all suffer from the mistakes. It is not easy to be right every time!

Looking Forward

So, our elected leaders, government employees, economists and banks just have to be right, in order for the economy to run smoothly. In our history, we've seen tax increases at the wrong time, for example, that really stretched out the effects of the 1929 depression. More recently, there were some bad guesses on how technology stocks should be priced. The folks setting policy and laws just need to be right – a really tough task when you are talking about the country's economic future. This is beginning to sound like a pitch to you voters that that education and experience of elected leaders is extremely import. And, they need to be able to hire well-qualified employees that run the government, day to day. Yep, that's my pitch.

OK, so we can learn from our past experiences, but what is the path to economic prosperity at this point in time? To answer this question, I like to look at fundamentals. I like to ask questions such as:

- ❏ Why do we have jobs?
- ❏ Who can or should "create" the jobs?
- ❏ How do they get created?

❑ Can our economy, or any economy, really employ everyone?

An Overview of iEmployment

In the next chapter, I will set goals for reducing unemployment and poverty. Then I'll examine some of the fundamentals of employment. I think this is important, because it will help us understand better what might be possible, and what our goals should be. This will include a look at jobs and free market capitalism.

Chapter 4 includes a discussion of how we relate to the global economy. We'll then examine the role of government. The government has a significant role to play in successful economies. Specifically, it has the ability to set laws and policies that encourage investment and success in private enterprise. This includes tax rates, tax incentives, environmental regulations, etc.

Before getting to the discussion of solutions to our unemployment problems it is appropriate to first discuss the role of education. Education is of critical importance in the ability of the country to see a very large majority of its people gainfully, successfully employed. We, as a country, need to be concerned about the quality of the education being provided, and about the cost of higher education. We also need to recognize that not everyone needs to go on the higher education path, and that trade skill education plays an important role in the development of our economy. We're going to argue that we should, in fact, bring manufacturing "back" to the U.S., a process that will place real value on trade skills.

Then, by way of setting the stage for looking into

solutions, a review of the impact of the housing bubble is appropriate.

This will lead up to the chapter on the "Development of an Impoverished Society." You might wonder why I'm effectively calling the U.S. economy an "Impoverished Society." I don't mean to make light of other nations of the world that have severe poverty problems, but I think we need to realize that we do have significant poverty[4] in the U.S., and that we ought to be trying to reduce/eliminate it.

What we're talking about here is the core process, critical to understanding in order to proceed forward. The goal then is to have an economy where nearly all can participate (have a job). Generally one cannot just walk out and declare – "I've got a job or I want a job – give it to me." It usually takes people to start up and/or expand an organization to hire folks to create goods and services for which there is demand. Again, generally, it also takes investment to create and grow these organizations.

For a society that is in trouble, it is going to take investment to develop the economy, either to expand existing entities or create new ones, in both cases based on actual or perceived demand for goods and services in the marketplace. In a free market system, private (instead of government) investment works best, in that incentives drive the organizations to succeed.

You might ask, "You mean we have to sit back and wait for people to invest to develop the economy?" In a sense,

---

[4] In 2012 we have about 15.5% of our population living in poverty, according to Associated Press surveys. That equates to about 46 million people.

that's right. There is no one single "magic bullet" that will suddenly cure our job problems. Getting investments going is a complex issue. As we will further discuss, there are a lot of factors that influence this process. They include but are not limited to:

- ❏ Personal income tax rates (affecting those small business people whose business is taxed as part of their personal income)
- ❏ Capital gains tax rates (that can strongly inhibit investment where it is needed)
- ❏ Corporate income tax rates (higher rates can reduce profits, that in turn reduce funds available for growth)
- ❏ Foreign competition (especially from countries that "dump" their products into our country[5])
- ❏ Foreign outsourcing (that has U.S. companies shipping manufacturing jobs overseas)
- ❏ Environmental protection rules and processes (that can delay and/or prohibit development)

The above begin to illustrate the complexity of the economic development process. Investors have to be willing to take risk, and can be deterred by any or all of the above factors. There are many factors that go into creating an environment that encourages development. So, when you are evaluating the worthiness of a candidate for a legislative

---

[5] When it comes to foreign competition, we cannot allow other countries to "dump" products into the U.S. market, i.e. sell products that are priced well below market by the use of artificial exchange rates and/or unreasonably low labor costs.

office, for example, don't expect a single, "Here's my single idea to create jobs." Look instead for understanding of the entire job creation process in our free market capitalistic system. Such a person will have a much better chance of success. Be they Republican, Democrat or Independent, if they understand the process, they can help solve the problem.

The suggested development process carries with it ramifications that need to be discussed. That includes private sector investment, infrastructure and energy and a serious look at the Living Wage Benefit.

The Living Wage Benefit that I am proposing sounds, on the surface, like a social justice issue. I present the case that the Living Wage Benefit has strong financial implications, and is really a very important part of any economic recovery plan.

A complex process can have all sorts of side effects, some of which are tough to handle. They get covered in the subsequent chapters, until we finally arrive at Chapter 23, a summary of my thoughts for developing the economy to create jobs.

2...Setting Goals

===

On Setting Goals

In the foregoing introduction, I have outlined the contents of this book and have introduced some of the concepts that I believe will be effective in solving the unemployment problem in this country. Before going into details of this program, it would be appropriate to set goals in place with regard to achieving economic recovery.

Providing Employment

Our primary goal should be to eliminate under-employment. While accurate statistics are difficult to come by, our country currently has a population of approximately 312 million people. The government considers that of these people, the potential workforce is about 155 million. At 19% real unemployment that means that 31 million people are without work or working part-time while seeking full-time work. If we set a goal of 4% real unemployment that means that we need to find work for 25 million people. At 4% real unemployment, we will be close to historical low unemployment rates. It is difficult to do much better because of normal job turnover. Lowering real unemployment to 4% will therefore be our goal.

Providing Living Wages

A second goal that should be undertaken is to reduce and/or eliminate poverty in the U.S. (In many areas of the country a job paying minimum wage puts you below the poverty line.) In achieving the goal of finding employment for these 25 million people, we also need to consider their wage levels. So, as part of this program we will set out a second goal, and that is to move gradually towards achieving Living Wages for full-time workers.

In setting this goal I do not suggest that the government pass laws or set up regulations that require companies to pay Living Wages to all of their full-time employees. Such a program will have the effect of reducing employment, particularly for younger, unskilled individuals.

I cover the subject of the Living Wage more thoroughly in Chapter 11 of this book, but I believe that this is an important goal that goes along with solving the un-employment problem. For many, the Living Wage concept is a social justice issue, but I suggest that it is in fact an important aspect of moving towards a stronger economy and employing the underemployed.

Resulting Tax Revenues

It is interesting to note what effect this additional employment will have on the economy. If we assume that the average wage for these 25 million people is $50,000 per year, then the payroll for these individuals amounts to $1.250 billion per year. If we assume that these individuals will pay income tax to the tune of approximately 15%, then the federal government will bring in approximately $187.5 billion per year in tax revenue. We have seen much discussion at the national level on the effect of tax increases and expense cuts, and they are usually measured over a 10-year period. So we can say that if we were successful in employing these 25 million people we would bring in a minimum of $1.875 trillion of additional revenue to the federal government coffers over the next 10 years.

The above calculates the contribution in taxes to the federal government that accrue only from income taxes levied against the 25 million new workers. There will be an additional tax revenue increase due to the increased level of revenues (and thus profitability) of the companies employing these people. While the above may excite the government big spenders, history has shown that accomplishing such goals generally results in lower tax rates.

3...Jobs and Free Market Capitalism

In the Beginning

In the process of looking at how jobs are created under free market capitalism it's useful to look back to the origins of societies. If we think back to the beginning of humankind we can envision that men/women were self-sufficient for themselves and/or their families. He/she was the hunter, the gatherer and the maker of clothes in order to survive. As societies developed and groups of individuals lived together the responsibilities for various jobs were shared.

Thus began an age of specialization where one individual might be the hunter for a group of individuals, another might gather, and another might make clothes. At some point a barter system developed that allowed members to obtain goods and services from other members on a fair basis. Finally, a monetary system came into being with the use of coinage to pay for goods and services, eliminating the need for direct trading; thus the beginnings of commerce.

Historically societies the world over have tried various forms of economic systems. Among those most recently tried are capitalism, socialism and communism. The free market capitalist system of the United States has proven to be a very successful economic model that has resulted in dramatic growth in this country. Capitalism has survived based in large part on the individual's need to strive for improvement in his/her life. Property ownership is also an important element in this drive to better oneself.

Commerce becomes more complicated when one moves beyond a small-contained society, such as a village or town. The concept of trading between societies emerges and introduces the possibility that some products may be produced in one society, and sold for the benefit of both societies. Such developments complicate the issue of how a society can employ all of its individuals in the normal course of events.

The U.S. has been very successful under free market capitalism, providing employment with fairly low un-employment rates, often approaching 4 to 5 percent. Our current economy has, to a certain extent, developed into a global economy with goods and services being traded worldwide, but as we shall discuss later, this global economy has had profound effect on our own economy and our ability to maintain high employment.

Free Market Capitalism

Fundamentally, a society survives by having its members working to provide goods and services for the benefit of all. The free market aspects of capitalism dictate what goods and services will be made available and at what prices. Supply and demand factor heavily into the equation and the economy thus becomes self-regulating. For example, if a certain service becomes very profitable, more individuals will enter into the market to provide that service. With the greater availability of those services, a fixed demand and prices for services in decline due to the competition, the market becomes less attractive for individuals to enter. This self-regulation of supply and demand usually results in a balanced economic environment.

In the simplest model, a society may be composed of individuals providing goods and services. As the demand for more sophisticated goods and services developed it became necessary for groups of individuals to work together to provide these goods and services. Thus the concept of a corporation emerged. A corporation is basically an entity formed to provide goods and services that man alone cannot provide. The corporation, of course, provides employment opportunities for many.

Any modern economy under the free market capitalist system requires that balance be maintained between the supply of and the demand for labor. In the history of the world, there have been many times when the supply of labor far exceeded the demand and individuals or larger entities were able to obtain very low cost labor in order to accomplish their goals of profitably providing goods and services. The extreme example of this out of balance condition, of course, is slavery, a very common condition in the past but now seriously frowned upon by society.

While most societies may have eliminated slavery in most parts of the world there are still areas where the supply of labor far exceeds the demand; and as a result employees receive very low wages. This is very common in developing countries and as we will see later represents a real problem in trying to find balance in a particular society, so that most if not all of the members of the society have gainful employment. For example, in the case of China, its huge population means that goods and services can be provided with very low labor cost, allowing companies in China to provide goods to others in the world at below competitive pricing.

From this discussion we can say that achieving balance of employment in a society is a nontrivial task. It involves balancing the supply and demand of labor within the society, but also in other societies that may be competing to provide goods and services. This often has resulted in the imposition of import tariffs in order to create trade barriers. Trade wars can result. Solving these issues is an important and continuing task.

The United States has historically navigated through these trade problems, sometimes with difficulty, but in the end achieving a balanced economy. Our current economy however, is not in balance (as evidenced by the very high foreign trade imbalance), and we thus have very high unemployment.

As previously discussed, part of the problem has occurred because of our own actions taken by our government and private industry, resulting in the housing bubble and subsequent financial crisis. But it is also the result of a gradually expanding tendency on the part of companies within the United States to outsource manufacturing jobs to foreign countries that have significantly lower labor costs. This has been going on for a long time, and has been continued in the belief that fair trading between countries will provide the opportunity for the United States to manufacture and export goods and services in balance with its imports. Unfortunately this has not come to pass. We now have a severe trade imbalance with imports far exceeding exports.

Of course, energy dependence on foreign oil imports is a significant part of the problem.[6]

Those That Create Jobs

In the foregoing, I talked of jobs being created by individuals and by corporations. At this point it is worth looking at the various forms of entities that provide jobs and look at the factors that influence their ability to operate in the United States. Job creating entities include individuals, both technical and professional, partnerships, limited partnerships, and corporations. Each has a unique role to play in our commerce.

It is important to understand the structure and to understand the motivations folks have for taking (sometimes very high) risks to achieve significant gain. To the extent that the work required to create and/or manufacture products cannot be achieved solely by individuals, then corporations are usually formed. These entities can then provide significant job opportunities. Therefore, when looking at unemployment problems it is important to understand how these various entities will hire people and how they will compensate them.

Individuals typically operate alone or as a sole proprietorship. They are typically formed based on skills possessed by the individual. These entities typically represent formation of business with the least amount of capital required. The motivation to form the entities may include a

---

[6] The trade imbalance was estimated to be in excess of $500 Billion in 2012. In 2011, the deficit with China alone was approximately $295 Billion.

strong interest in working for oneself or the belief that a unique opportunity exists by which the individual can gain significant monetary reward. Where capital investment is required, the individual expects to achieve a return on that investment that is much better than he can achieve from a bank savings account, for example. These entities are typically taxed as part of the individual's income tax return and they often employ others. We call them small businesses and they account for a very significant percentage of employment in the U.S.

Partnerships obviously involve more than one individual and the business entity is formed when just one individual cannot achieve the business goals. Here the required investment may be larger. Many partnerships are professional partnerships, such as law firms, medical firms, etc. The capital required to form such entities obviously varies depending upon the business purpose, and is usually more than that required for an individual. Partnership profits usually show on each partner's income tax form, spread proportional to the percent ownership of each partner.

As stated, corporations are formed to accomplish goals that typically cannot be accomplished by an individual. The implication is that to be effective, the company must hire a significant number of people in order to achieve its business objectives.

Individuals can finance corporations, but venture capitalists and/or other shareholders typically finance the larger corporations. Typically, individuals with a common interest form corporations. They may have as their principal objective monetary reward or the accomplishment of some worthwhile benefit to society. In other words, they perceive that there is a market need. As Henry Kaiser said regarding his business philosophy, "Find a need and fill it."

Corporations typically require significant investment. The founders often make the initial investment and venture capitalists may be called upon to provide additional funding. The founders and the venture capitalists expect a significant return on their investment for the risk taken. Returns are usually realized by taking the corporation public or by merger into another larger corporation.[7]

As we will see later, perceived availability of liquidity by one of these means is key to encouraging individuals to make investments in the first place. No one wants to invest in a company with no obvious means of eventually realizing gains if the company is successful. As a result, government laws, tax rates and policies and regulations can have a profound effect on whether one believes they will eventually see profitable liquidity.

Corporations, then, are typically owned by shareholders (the founders and outside investors) and are governed by the bylaws of the company. In most states bylaws require that the corporation must meet its fiduciary responsibilities to the shareholders. That's an elaborate way of saying that the corporations (unless they're nonprofit) need to be profitable and need to maximize financial performance for the benefit of shareholders.

The public usually holds the stock in mature corporations. The public investor is willing to pay some

---

[7] As I will cover in a later chapter, regulations such as those set in place by the Sarbanes-Oxley legislation have dampened many company's goals of going public.

multiple of the reported or expected annual earnings (commonly referred to as the price to earnings ratio) when trading the stock. This multiple is typically calculated based on the perceived ability of the Corporation to pay dividends (whether or not they actually pay dividends). The multiple that a given stock achieves in the market is then a function of the earnings (profits) of the company and the perceived ability to grow.

The bottom line of all this discussion is that our country needs to have a favorable set of economic and social conditions that lead potential investors to validly perceive that the risk of investment is worth taking in pursuit of rewards.

The Large Corporation

One often hears complaints about the nature of large corporations and the supposition that their main goal is to have the lowest possible rate of compensation for their employees for the benefit of the corporation's profits. The corporation is therefore often viewed to be in opposition to the common man.

I suggest that corporations, in fact, provide an excellent opportunity for individuals, including the opportunity for advancement within the corporate structure, along with the attendant increase in wages. People manage corporations, just as they manage small businesses. As in all parts of our society, there is no guarantee that your boss will be the ideal manager. The beauty of the free enterprise system is that the employee, if up against a bad situation, is free to move to different parts of the corporation or different corporations altogether. Again supply and demand is at work to protect the individual. In the current environment the risk in moving to a new job is high due to the high unemployment rate.

In most forms of private enterprise some investment is required on the part of the individuals and/or stockholders in order to create and/or expand the business. Such investments will be made when market opportunities are present. If we are to solve the unemployment problem we must therefore look to the motivation on the part of the investors. Specifically, we need to look at the risk/reward factors. If we can create an environment in which the risk/reward ratio is correct, we will see additional investment and thus we will see the creation of additional jobs through the creation/expansion process.

It is one thing to say that a favorable environment exists in order for investors take risk, but is likewise important that markets exist that provide the opportunity for these individuals to create or expand their businesses. In the United States more than half of the potential market for goods and services comes from the individuals living and working in the country. The ability of these individuals to be in the position to be part of the market implies that individuals are being paid wages sufficiently high to allow them to make purchases.

Thus, there is a very strong coupling between the presence of a market for goods and services and the extent to which employees are well compensated for their work. In other words, if corporations and individuals pay their employees a Living Wage they will be contributing to the size of the market for their goods and services. This positive feedback is often overlooked in our economy, but it is an important contributor to solving the unemployment problem. In chapter 11 I will further expand the concept of the Living Wage as it applies to solving the problem of unemployment in an impoverished society.

To illustrate this point, consider the following. I toured parts of China in 2004 and learned that the Chinese Government faced the problem of lacking a middle class that could purchase goods made in China. They solved the problem, in part, by allowing middle level government workers to charge and keep fees for issuing permits for various types of purchases (all controlled by the government). This policy crated a middle class, with wages sufficient for them to become part of the market. It's kind of a roundabout way of allowing some to earn Living Wages. It does illustrate the point that a country needs to have workers that can afford to buy goods and services that they create. Otherwise, there is no domestic market and the country must try to succeed largely in the export business.

A Look at the Process – a Startup

Since we've been discussing the types of entities that employ people in our society, it might be useful to look at the process for starting up a company. In the following I'll go through some of the details, and in the process, note the effects of outside conditions, such as interest rates and policies and regulations.

For starters, let's pick the area around Stockton, California. This area has a very high underemployment rate (greater than 20%) and the City of Stockton has just filed bankruptcy proceedings. Further, let's decide that with the labor availability, and the proximity to the Great California Central Valley, that we'll start up a clothing manufacturing company. Let's assume that we have a large, nationwide clothing retailer lined up to purchase our line of clothing provided that the cost is right. I'll discuss more later on conceptual problems in competing with low labor cost.

OK, first we'll pull together a founding team, experienced in clothing manufacturing, and in company financial matters, including the experience and ability to raise funds for this startup. The team then needs to come up with a business plan, one that will lead to a profitable operation and that will eventually lead to a way for the founders, investors and employees (often via stock options) to achieve liquidity (possibly by going public or by merging out to a larger company). At this stage, we have to consider the following:

- ❑ Availability of funds from potential investors. A real key here to possible success. Potential investors, such as venture capitalists, need to see an investment friendly environment. That includes favorable long term capital gains tax rates, and a consistent outlook to the future (one year low rates, for example, discourage investment).

- ❑ Interest rates for possible loans. At some point in the company's evolution, lines of credit from commercial banks may prove useful in growing the company (utilizing collateralized lending based on assets like receivables, for example). Reasonable interest rates are thus important.

- ❑ Corporate tax rates. Ideally, the company would face reasonable corporate tax rates. Currently, the U.S. has one of the highest maximum corporate tax rates in the world. This just raises the bar on the difficulty in achieving good earnings. With high corporate tax rates, companies must raise prices in order to remain properly profitable. This puts the company in a bad position with respect to competition. Also, as has been reported in the popular media in recent years, high corporate tax rates encourage companies to keep their cash from international sales in foreign countries that have lower corporate tax rates.

❏ Capital gains tax rates. As previously mentioned, lower long term capital gains taxes are an incentive for investment, which we need to get this company going.

❏ Conditions for granting stock options to employees. For many years, companies could issue stock options to employees wherein the potential gain from such options did not represent compensation to the employee. Then, a few years ago, the financial accounting board in the U.S decided that those potential gains should be counted as company expense at the time of grant. This, as with high corporate tax rates, lowers the earnings of the company for a given price position in the markets they serve. Stock options have in the past been a very successful incentive for employees for working hard to achieve the goals of the company. The accounting change has greatly reduced the granting of options.

❏ Burden of becoming a public company. Whereas our company will be private early on, we will likely need to structure our accounting so as to allow the company to go public in the future. Congress's passage of the Sarbanes-Oxley Act in July of 2002 radically changed the accounting rules for public companies, adding an increasing burden on the companies, and again reducing earnings for given price points in the market for their goods and services.

The law was passed in reaction to accounting problems at Enron and Tyco International and a few other firms.   The tendency of our congress, supported by some voters, to always want to pass new laws and new regulations each time someone screws up big-time places an ever increasing cost burden on companies in the U.S.   This, at a time when we face global competition for manufactured goods, wherein labor costs of the foreign suppliers are often well below our own.[8]

❑   <u>Foreign outsourcing and import competition</u>.   In consideration of starting a clothing manufacturing business, foreign outsourcing and import competition are matters of serious concern in a competitive marketplace.   These factors will have major impact on the willingness of anyone to invest in the company.

There are at least two activities we can embrace to mitigate the problem.   First, since we are starting up a new clothing manufacturing company, we need to purchase and employ the latest in modern manu-

---

[8] It is noteworthy that Enron failed because of its accounting problems, and brought down Arthur Anderson & Co. with it.   The failures did not require establishment of any new regulations or laws! When people make errors, the economic system responds.

facturing tooling. This may provide a significant competitive edge by achieving greatly enhanced productivity. Second, we need the U.S. government to be diligent in protecting our companies from the "dumping" of goods manufactured by foreign manufacturers.

In the end, voters need to decide if the down side of outsourcing (loss of jobs in the U.S.) will motivate them to vote by exercising their purchasing power (as in buy Made in the U.S.A.). This is a tough issue, but one that must be solved if we are to return to normal employment in the U.S.

❑ <u>Availability of skilled work force</u>. We've chosen the Stockton area of California as our factory location, in part based on an available workforce. We may have an issue of employee training to contend with. We're not worried so much about engineers and managers as we are about skilled equipment operators in the clothing field. Here is an opportunity for the government, through its taxation program, to provide tax incentives for training that is carried out by companies. This is an important obstacle that must be overcome as we try to put everyone back to work.

Assuming we get through that planning phase, and have lined up funding, conditional on our ability to locate the company in the planned area, lets look at the next set of potential obstacles.

❑ <u>Land availability</u>. In this startup we will need a manufacturing facility, and since it is of a special nature, we will assume we need to start by purchasing

land.   In doing so, we need the availability of
infrastructure, as in roads, water, sewer, etc. Here is
where the government has a role, including Federal,
State and local agencies. We will be letting no-growth
advocates have their say, but we need local
governments to handle these discussions in a timely
manner.

❑   Environmental impact of the business. We will likely
    need to do an environmental impact report on the
    proposed facility. Here again, the government needs
    to have a pro-growth jobs attitude. This is a tough
    area. One can expect resistance from environmental
    groups, especially if they are opposed to most
    development.   If opposed, they will typically use
    every excuse to slow down or stop the process. They
    need to have their say, but well organized and
    managed local and state governments can facilitate
    the process by adhering to the legal process and being
    sure that all parties do the same.

❑   Air quality considerations.   The Stockton area has
    well known air quality problems. The new plant must
    adhere to the air quality regulations. The question to
    ask is, "Is this the time to set up new policies with
    tighter restrictions, that could preclude establishment
    of the company, or is there a reasonable way for all
    involved to compromise?"

❑   Building permits and regulations.   Building permits
    will be required.   Recent history shows tighter and
    tighter building policies being put into place, certainly
    in California. These need to be balanced against the
    need for solving the unemployment problem.

❑   <u>Going "Green" requirements</u>. Because of the fear of the consequences of man-made "global warming," we see more and more policies pushing towards "going green." These activities can increase costs of operation and induce delays in getting our plant completed. My question; "Is this the time to force Green concepts?" Placing implementation of these concepts ahead of providing employment for people is bothersome, if not downright wrong.

As can be seen from the above, starting a company is a complex process. The benefit will be increased employment, but regulations and policies set forth by our governments (Federal, State and Local) must be geared to support such growth. These policies and regulations can have a profound effect on the ability of entrepreneurs to start up new companies. Our elected officials need to understand the entrepreneurial process in order to govern effectively in support of increased economic activity, in turn, to support job growth. Here is an opportunity to vote for those that understand the process.

A Look at the Expansion Process

Now let's take a look at the process for expanding a business that is up and running, and that sees the need to expand to better take advantage of market demand. This approach is often touted as the quick fix to the job market.

First, consider how fast a company can grow utilizing its own internal financial resources. Generally, companies can grow at a rate equal to their generated return on equity. The limitation is caused by the need for cash to support higher levels of inventory and higher levels of receivables associated with growth. So, if a company can achieve a return on equity of around 20%, then it can increase revenues by about 20% per year, assuming it does not have excessive inventory or cash reserves.

The return on equity is a direct function of the profitability of the company, so factors that detract from profitability detract from its growth rate. This is again where the financial atmosphere in the country can have a direct influence on the ability of companies to grow, and therefore hire more people. Tax rates, both corporate and individual, clearly affect company profitability, and thus affect a company's ability to hire additional people, assuming there is market demand for their products.

The need for increased financial resources in order to expand a business applies to small businesses[9] and large corporations. This is a key factor in developing the economy. Someone must decide to invest if an operation is to grow. High tax rates, both personal and corporate, inhibit growth by diverting funds to the government that could otherwise support growth.

Market demand for products is clearly a primary driver of growth for a company. This brings us back to the point – domestic demand for products is a major factor in leading job growth. Conversion of jobs from foreign outsourcing to domestic hiring can clearly also drive job growth. For the

---

[9] Small business taxes are often paid as part of the owner's income tax. Here then, individual income tax rates are very important. High tax rates will automatically limit funds available to support growth, and thus provide more jobs.

same level of production, more people are employed in the U.S., driving more demand for products in general.

A third source of market demand occurs when a company can increase its exports to other countries. This latter point was often made when political talk centered on free trade agreements. We were told that by having free trade agreements, we would increase exports of U.S. products, thus improving our own economic situation. As it turned out, companies, and high tech companies in particular, are able to increase sales to foreign countries, but these companies have turned to foreign outsourcing for manufacturing, leaving our country without the benefit of increased employment. We need to re-look at the effect of free trade agreements when manufacturing jobs are outsourced.

Finally, if the projected market demand is sufficient, a company will want to grow faster than can be achieved utilizing internal financial resources. In this case, the company may look to outside sources of funding, such as banking relationships or new equity investments or the sale of bonds. Here again the financial condition of the country is important so that the company will be in a position to raise additional funds to support the increased growth. Having an atmosphere of stability in terms of interest rates and tax rates enhances the financial condition of the country.

The Independent Entrepreneur

At the other end of the spectrum we find the independent small business entrepreneur. These individuals typically risk their own money when starting up businesses. It is also not uncommon for such individuals to borrow money in order to fund their startups and expansion plans. These individuals are a major source of employment opportunity in the United States. They take the risk of starting their own business, motivated in part to work for themselves and in part to maintain a profitable business.[10]

These independent people are to truly be admired. When you see a van driving down the road with an ad on the side describing Joe's Fix It business or Harry's Gutter Cleaning business, have you ever thought about the risk that Joe or Harry have taken in order to start and maintain their businesses? You see these folks everywhere and they provide a very large portion of total employment in the United States.

These folks are taxed, typically, as part of their own personal income. Therefore, when personal income tax rates are high, the individuals have less money available for expansion, should they see the market demand. Again, when we as a country debate personal income and corporate income tax rates, we need to realize who is paying the taxes, and what effect tax increases, for example, will have on the ability of the individuals or corporations to expand their business and thus hire additional people. This is the primary motivation to not raise income taxes on these individuals during a time when we are looking for these folks to expand their businesses to provide more jobs.

---

[10] According to the U.S. Government's Small Business Administration, small businesses (those employing less that 500 people) account for 49% of private sector employment and 42% of the private sector payroll.

iEmployment

4…Relating to the Global Economy

The Global Economy

In the foregoing, I made an assumption that should be pursued further. Specifically, I suggested that an economy in balance under free market capitalism would provide employment opportunity for essentially all that are willing to work. The question; is this really true?

When we talk of the global economy, we are essentially saying that the world is one society, that we have common interests. From the social viewpoint that may be something we strive for, but economically such a statement needs to be examined.

In the previous chapter I discussed the history of man, so to speak. I think the rationale that we could define a village as a society is reasonable. But what happens as we expand our scope. As we expand our view (using U.S. terminology), we go through towns, cities, states, regions, countries, continents and then the world. The question is, "As we expand the size of the society geographically, can we use the same rules and definitions from the economic viewpoint?"

We, in this country, are certainly comfortable going to the country level economically. We have operated as a single society since the founding of the country (with a few exceptions, such as the civil war). We have no problem in letting goods and services cross state lines. For example, we don't expect every state to manufacture automobiles, and not all can be agriculturally strong like California. Part of our comfort comes from the availability of transportation, part from common language, and common currency.

Success Beyond the Country Level

So, the question is, "What happens when we go to continental, and finally global? Are we still comfortable in saying that these two steps are consistent with a common economic society?" Interestingly, we don't seem to have much of a problem from the continent viewpoint in accepting Canada.[11] I believe at least part of the reason is based on their economy being similar to ours. That is, their standard of living is probably even with the U.S.

Including Mexico, on the other hand, is a little more problematic. Mexico's economic state is not even with ours as regards the standard of living. This puts their cost of available labor well below ours and presents problems with respect to competition. Outsourcing to Mexico feeds our unemployment problem.

The next step, to global, produces varied results. First, we have a history of successful competition with European countries. We have imported goods from them for years, and we export to them. These goods have been competitive with U.S. made products and result in a healthy global

---

[11] On January 1, 1994, the North American Free Trade Agreement between the United States, Canada, and Mexico (NAFTA) entered into force. Source: U.S. Government

competition.   Examples include automobiles such as Mercedes, Volvo and Volkswagen. They include wines from France, baked goods from Belgium and industrial equipment from Germany. Such import activity lets Europe be part of our economic society because Europe's standard of living, and therefore cost of labor, fits well with ours.

We have also successfully imported goods from Japan including high quality automobiles. The beginning phase of auto imports was not so smooth in the 1960's. Japan worked a price advantage with low cost labor and low quality in the early phase. In recent years, the labor costs are more aligned with ours, and Japan realized the need for quality.

So, we can identify successful global commerce. The common denominator that makes the global economy work is the standard of living amongst the countries. This keeps the cost of labor competitive, and gives buyers in all countries the freedom to buy products manufactured outside their own country. Not to say that there have not been problems. It takes a lot of work to implement free trade between countries. There is always a temptation to protect one's own products.

More Difficult Areas of Trade

The above shows that we can successfully extend our concept of society from the economic viewpoint to the global level for at least some countries. But, there are countries of the world where we encounter difficulty. The difficulty centers on the standard of living in many countries, which results in very low labor costs. These countries are problematic. We end up with significant outsourcing to some of these countries, thereby damaging our domestic employment opportunities.

We are told by economists and elected officials that the global economy is the answer, regardless of these problems. I suggest that the problems are real, and are resulting in an underemployment problem in the U.S. that is going to be very difficult to solve.

Consider the scenario put forth by the experts. We can outsource our manufacturing because we can adjust our economy to be more service oriented. OK, let's accept that premise. Then, let's look at how we can balance trade between such countries. It's clear that the manufacturing can be outsourced. To achieve balance of trade then, we need to export something to the manufacturing countries. Since we outsourced manufacturing, I guess we will export services!

But how do we export accounting, or healthcare, or other services. We have a geographic barrier. We have a language barrier. True, modern communication via the Internet is a big help, but I suggest there are fundamental limits as to how we can balance trade, even with improved communication. As I've said throughout this book, these developing countries need to get their own economies going if they are to fairly enter the global economy. It's not clear that exports based on low cost labor will result in development of their economies. It certainly will allow companies, here and abroad, to gain a competitive advantage in the world markets, at the expense of underpaid workers in those countries.

5...Role of the Government

Regulations and Policies

Given the nature of free enterprise, as described in the foregoing, one might logically ask, "What is the role of the government in trying to solve unemployment problems?" According to the preamble to the Constitution, the responsibilities of the federal government in general are:

1. In Order to form a more perfect Union,

2. establish Justice,

3. insure domestic Tranquility,

4. provide for the common Defense

5. promote the general Welfare

6. secure the Blessings of Liberty to ourselves and our posterity

While these might be the primary responsibilities of the federal government, the government is also in the position of setting policies and passing laws, which can have a profound effect on private enterprise. The federal government clearly guides and constrains free enterprise in our free market capitalistic system.

It is clear that over time the federal government has grown and has taken a more and more onerous position with respect to trying to guide and control private enterprise.[12] There are some aspects of this activity that are worthwhile and there are some that excessively constrain the development of private enterprise. Some of the positive aspects of federal government involvement in private enterprise include the following.

- ❑ Infrastructure. Clearly, both federal and state governments have a significant role to play in the development of infrastructure in our society. The role is defined based on the fact that the infrastructure is generally for the benefit of all living in a given area and therefore rightly can benefit from taxation of all living within the area be it local, state or federal.

- ❑ Financial regulation. The government typically has a legitimate role in financial regulation of banks and other financial institutions. That includes the stock markets as well. The general population benefits from these regulations from the viewpoint of protection from fraud and the achievement of fair and consistent regulations.

- ❑ Taxation. In order to finance its other activities, governments typically levy taxes on the income of individuals and corporations, and on the sale of goods and services. How these taxes are structured and put into effect can have a serious effect on the ability of private enterprise to get investors to take

---

[12] Federal employment grew 13% — 250,000 jobs — from the recession's start in December 2007 to a peak in September of 2012. During that time, private employment fell 5% and state and local governments cut staffs by 2%. Source: USA Today

the risks necessary to invest to expand the economy.

❏ <u>Other regulations</u>.   One can also find appropriate
   regulations among the myriad of local, state and
   federal regulations. As we shall discuss, these are not
   always a positive influence on the ability to develop
   the economy.

Taxation

Taxation is one of the strongest influences on investors
in their willingness to take the risk of investing to expand
existing or to start new businesses. In the popular press there
is a continuing debate as to the influence of income and
capital gains tax rates and how they might affect the
economy. Fortunately, we have a history to rely on that
shows the influence of tax rates on the willingness of
investors to take risk.[13]

One of the best examples of the effects of taxation
occurred in 1979 when the federal legislature revised the
capital gains tax rate in the downward direction. Prior to this
change the stock market was basically not supporting new
stock issues because of a lack of investor interest.

Once the capital gains rate was significantly lowered the
investors came back into the market and the opportunity for
companies to go public was revived. Once investors saw that
their private investments could be taken public they realized
that they had a means of liquidation of their otherwise illiquid

---

[13] The history of long term capital gains tax rates in the U.S. is
amazing, varying from the highest rates of 77% to 12.5% in the 1920's.
The maximum rate was 15% under the Bush tax cuts.   Source: Citizens
for Tax Justice, November 2011.

private investments. That realization resulted in increased venture capital investment and therefore growth of the economy.

Tax Rate Stability

The issue of taxation and specifically tax rates is complex. Not only must one have favorable rates, but one must also have confidence in the stability of these rates in the future. If one is to undertake the risk of investment, short-term changes in income or capital gains rates will have a negative impact on the willingness of investors to invest.

For example, capital gains tax rates were set at 20% (maximum rate for individuals with more than $400,000 income) at the end on 2012. Along with the increase to the maximum 20%, the Affordable Care Act tax increase of 3.8% put the total capital gains tax rate at 23.8% as of January 1, 2013. These recent tax increases are not going to improve the environment for investors for making investments to help develop our economy, and growth will be inhibited. Living with the uncertainty of how these rates might change, often within 6 months, severely complicates the investment decisions and delays actions that would grow the economy.

Healthcare Uncertainty

Uncertainty has also been introduced with passage of the Affordable Care Act. The uncertainty centers on what additional costs companies may incur and how they will need to restructure their healthcare benefits. The uncertainty comes at the worst time when we are trying to encourage investments in our economy to provide growth.

Other Regulations and Policies

The ability of the federal government to issue other policies, regulations and laws can also have a profound effect on the willingness of investors to make the investments necessary to expand the economy and thus begin to solve the unemployment problem. Many times these rules are set forth to achieve some admirable goal, but have the unintended consequence of restricting the economy by discouraging investment.

In chapters 19 and 20 I will discuss two of the most influential areas, that of environmental protection[14] and global warming. Both of these areas are having a significant effect on the willingness of investors to take risk and make their investments.

The country faces a dilemma with respect to these regulations. On the one hand, many are anxious to enforce regulations with respect to environmental protection and reduction of man-made global warming. But in doing so at a time of severe underemployment, they are in fact inhibiting the growth of the economy. It is as though one would like to postpone some of the regulations to a time when we can more readily accomplish said regulations without destroying the economy.

In summary, local, state and federal governments can and do have a serious effect on the ability of the country to accomplish economic growth that will solve the unemploy-

---

[14] The EPA was established by the Environment Protection Act of 1997. So, we have tighter regulations going into effect just when we are foreign outsourcing jobs and getting ready to create the housing bubble and subsequent collapse. This is beginning to sound like a perfect storm!

ment problem. It suggests that it is time to revise thinking with respect to these regulations.[15] In the past developments could be approved only after consideration of the environmental effects. In the future it makes sense to say that new environmental regulations can be put into effect only after consideration of their effects on the economy. The subject here is, after all, discussion of how to create jobs in order to mitigate and/or eliminate poverty.

Solving this problem of underemployment is the single most important task that the country can undertake at this time. We cannot afford to leave people in poverty for an extended period of time, which is what is happening at present. It is not only morally irresponsible; it is destructive to the basic fabric of our society.

Priorities

Many will say that our actions in the past have led us into this environmental position, that we cannot continue as in the past, but must take action now to prevent additional erosion of the environment. I say that is an admirable goal, but that trying to correct this all at once is occurring at the expense of the well being of our citizens. We need to strike a balance here if we are to make progress in solving the unemployment problem.

In my career in Silicon Valley I encountered a similar problem. It's very simple. When you start a company you

---

[15] In 2012 the California Legislature tabled debate on SB 317, which would have repealed some of the more restrictive aspects of the California Environmental Quality Act of 1970. The need is recognized but not all are in agreement. The failure to correct these excesses just further delays economic recovery.

want to lay out your goals and objectives. Let's say you have an admirable goal in mind that will benefit society. At the same time the startup company is intended to make a profit for its shareholders. So how do we state our primary mission? Do we first state that we want to achieve our admirable goals and then yes, we want to be profitable, or do we state that we first want to be profitable, so that we will be able to achieve our admirable goals?

In this case our business sense told us that we needed to put profits first in order to be able to afford achievement of the admirable goals. In this business example profitable operation would in fact enhance the ability of the company to achieve its more admirable goals. I believe the same can be said for the perceived environmental problems in our country. If we put development of the economy first, we will expand the economy and this will give us additional resources that we would otherwise not have to work on environmental problems.

6...The Role of Education

A Critical Need

Before we get to the discussion of specific actions that can be taken to mitigate and/or eliminate our unemployment problem we need to talk about the role of education. Most will agree that a good education is key to achieving satisfactory employment in our society.

There has been considerable discussion at the national level on the relative merits and/or demerits of our educational system.[16] I will not attempt to contribute to that debate, but it is an extensive and serious problem that should be addressed. However, education plays an important role in the development of an economy. Very simply stated, one needs well-educated employees for many of the job opportunities that will become available. As we will discuss in the chapter on the Living Wages, education is of primary importance in one's ability to achieve employment and a satisfying life.

---

[16] Federal Government Education Spending started out at the beginning of the 20th century at one percent of Gross Domestic Product (GDP). It currently runs at a rate of about six percent of GDP.

Service Oriented Economy?

When we discuss the need for excellent education in our country we need to have in mind the type of work that we expect to be available. It is often said that in our modern global economy, we are becoming service oriented as opposed to manufacturing oriented. If that were true, this would be reflected in different needs for education. It would imply that trade skills are of lesser importance and communication, economics and other skills are more important.

I'll discuss some aspects of this later in chapters on exporting jobs and importing goods from other countries, but I suggest that the statement that we must become a service oriented economy because we must let manufacturing jobs go overseas is not an appropriate statement. If we are to export most or all of our manufacturing to other countries, we will become out of balance with respect to our broad capabilities and could be placed in a vulnerable position with respect to certain critical manufacturing capabilities.

Basically we're back to a dilemma similar to that which was discussed with respect to the environment. That is, is it our responsibility to bring up the wealth of developing countries by shipping out our manufacturing jobs, or is it the responsibility of each country to develop their economies in a more balanced way? Once again, we're faced with choices.

When the move was made to export jobs over the last 20 or more years, and to accept more imports from foreign countries, manufacturers in this country put forth the argument that by allowing these imports with reciprocal trade agreements we would increase the market for our exports and would thus increase our exports and achieve a better balance of trade. The flaw in the argument occurred when we began to export our own manufacturing jobs instead of exporting the product. We thus have, and have had for some time, a severe balance of trade problem.

So, I suggest that we in fact need to have a more balanced economy and that we need to keep a significant amount of manufacturing at home. That, in turn, has influence on the type of educational system that we must have. It suggests specifically that we need to consider not only college education but technical skills education as well. This is more in line with countries in Europe, for example, where an individual is not stigmatized for not having gone to a four-year college. It suggests that we need to have trade schools that allow individuals to follow their interests in a way that will reward them with wages that will give them the life they desire.

Another problem that I suggest we need to address is the cost of higher education in this country. We are at the point where, without financial help, the cost of a college education is not necessarily commensurate with the return on the investment. Costs of college education are rising well above the rate of inflation. This suggests that we need to find a way to provide college education in a more cost effective way. It may turn out that the Internet may provide an answer to these cost issues in that the skills of a college professor can be greatly leveraged through education over the Internet. That's just one example of a possible way to solve the problem but it certainly needs to be addressed

Federal Role/Influence
I believe that the federal government does have a role in

working towards a better-educated population. What I'm going to suggest is probably not what you were thinking of, but I believe that if we are to achieve very low rates of underemployment, we need to focus on good education for a very large percentage of the population (less high school dropout, for example). How, might you ask, can the federal government influence this need?

The federal government, through its taxation policies and through its welfare and unemployment relief policies, has the opportunity to have a system in place wherein it is a significant advantage for couples to marry and remain married. A more wholesome home environment with appropriate adult role models has been shown to have a profound effect on the willingness of children to continue with their education.

Society in general can help with this problem, independent of the federal government by encouraging our young people to stay in school, but this idea of incentive encouragement may be an effective way to contribute to educational success.

On-the Job Training

Assuming one can devote the time and energy to a longer-term educational program, there are on-the-job training programs, often sponsored by local governments. For example, there are strict training requirements in place for individuals that would desire to work in utility plants.

An important part of the training that is required for individuals interested in such careers includes on-the-job experience. Private associations and government entities both offer training classes and private and public utilities will often employ trainees. Such hiring will enable them to gain the required experience in order to be properly licensed. These are examples of the kind of education that can be extremely valuable, even though they do not involve a college education.

In the current, post Great Recession environment we have a secondary problem. The unemployment situation has lasted sufficiently long that children of the underemployed are now growing up to the age where they should be taking additional schooling, either in trade schools, junior colleges, or colleges. Family funding for such education becomes much more difficult after such an extended economic recovery period.

One possible way to compensate for this problem is to provide companies tax credits for the costs of training individuals for jobs within their companies. Such a program could conceptually mitigate this lack of funding problem.

7...Impact of the Housing Bubble

The Escalation

In the late 1990's politicians in our country decided to try to expand homeownership to individuals and families with lower incomes. This led to a relaxation of the standards with respect to income requirements that were necessary in order to obtain a home mortgage.[17] Applications for home mortgages based on the relaxed standards (called sub prime mortgages) accepted by the banks resulted in a significant increase in home ownership. This raised the demand for housing in the United States and our free market system responded with higher prices for existing homes and a flurry of new home building.

This escalation of prices and home building activity, coupled with continued low interest rates for mortgages, produced an extremely active market for new and previously owned homes. The escalation of home prices was viewed by many to be the new paradigm. Buy a home and the value will always go higher! As a result, people were willing to pay

---

[17] The 1977 Community Reinvestment Act as modified under the Clinton administration triggered community outreach by banks, under pressure from various groups. That transformed mandatory credit issuance based not on credit worthiness, but on the basis of "fairness."

extremely high prices for homes when, in fact, the economics could not justify such high pricing.

This new paradigm might have continued had it not been for the credit problems associated with the sub prime mortgages. These mortgages represented a severe problem because the individuals who had been granted these mortgages were not necessarily in a position to continue the resulting high mortgage payments.

Banking and the commerce industry reacted to the sub prime lending problem by creating packages of high quality and sub prime mortgages to be resold to investors. There was a significant lack of due diligence exercised by these financial institutions and as folks began to realize that the sub prime mortgages were going to have a high degree of foreclosure rate, the market for these packaged loans began to collapse.

In the aftermath of this financial crisis, banks and brokerage houses were placed in a vulnerable position. Their difficulties led the way to a greatly weakened stock market, thus spreading the effect of these sub prime mortgages to non-associated victims such as those in retirement (with their savings placed in brokerage houses). The net result was a significant loss in the value of these retirement accounts and a general weakening of the economy.

The Housing Market Contraction

As prices for housing declined at a rapid rate the housing market for both new and previously owned homes collapsed. This affected the individuals who had purchased their homes, believing that they could afford them, and it had severe impact on the home construction business.

Since the peak of the market in 2006, we have seen record numbers of foreclosures and short sales. The government has attempted to soften the impact of these foreclosures by putting into place temporary financial facilities and regulations, but they've had little effect in helping those who fell victim to the sub prime lending mentality.

We have previously discussed the fact that the abrupt decline in the housing market resulted in a very large number of people suddenly becoming unemployed. This unemployment has lasted for a significant length of time, motivating the government to extend unemployment benefits two or more times to try to help these individuals through the crisis.

Even with the cessation of construction of new homes the market was saturated with homes, causing prices to slowly decline over what has now been a six-year period. This has left the construction industry in a very weakened condition, with many subcontractors and contractors closing down and/or filing for bankruptcy.[18]

The Recovery

One might have anticipated that with the readjustment of prices and the cessation of new home construction activity, the market would have recovered in a fairly short period of time, as has occurred in the past. This, however, had not occurred as of the end of 2012. At this time, economists believe that the existing home prices may have finally

---

[18] All told, it is estimated that some 8 million jobs were lost in the collapse of the housing market, just due to the reduction in construction activity.

bottomed out and there has been a minor increase in new home construction starts.

The recovery has been complicated by the government's tendency to always try to fix any problems that may occur in our economy. This time, the government reacted to the collapse, following the housing bubble, by implementing severely tightened lending requirements for homebuyers and initiating a significant increase in rules and regulations that have been placed on the banks.

Banks and other lending institutions were also not helped by changes in the accounting rules for public companies. Historically, these institutions were operating with accounting rules that allowed them to re-value their holdings over a period of time when market conditions drove values lower. Under the new "Mark to Market" rules, these write-downs were required to be taken promptly. The resulting lower evaluations of holdings forced many banks into takeover by the federal government.

So, rather than let the economy adapt to the housing bubble crisis, the government stepped in and tried to enforce its own ideas on how to correct the problem. The net result is a very restricted atmosphere for home mortgages, and this, in turn, is at least partially responsible for keeping the recovery of the housing market at a very low level.

A Solution to a Side Effect of the Crisis

One side effect of the collapse of the housing market concerns the credit ratings of individuals that purchased homes, undertaking sub prime mortgages. We cannot assume that all of these individuals were just talked into over-extending themselves in the housing market. There were a lot of home purchases that took place on the belief that this was the new paradigm for home pricing, that prices would continue to rise in the future. Okay, so this was a mistake on the part of those homebuyers, but it has disproportionate consequences for them in terms of their credit rating. For many it will be at least seven years before their credit rating can be completely restored and they can return to the housing market.

This suggests that there's an opportunity for private enterprise to put into place a type of Home Savings and Loan if you will, that deals in the financing of homes using lease/option buy programs. That is, there are large numbers of potential buyers for homes that have been burned by the sub-prime mortgage crisis, that have the resources to be able to purchase a home were it not for their damaged credit rating. It would seem to make sense to offer such individuals the opportunity of homeownership once again, by offering lease option buy programs. This would allow these individuals to begin a program of home ownership by at first leasing their home, with some portion of the payments going towards the eventual purchase of the home in later years.

Such a financial program has the advantage of restoring market demand for homes on an earlier time frame, thus accelerating the time to which normal building activity can resume. This will, of course, provide a significant increase in jobs in the U.S., which is our ultimate goal.

8...Development of an Impoverished Society

Are We Impoverished?

With the foregoing background, let's look at how we can go about the development of an impoverished Society. First, we need to define some of these terms.

- ❑ Society. A community, nation, or broad grouping of people having common traditions, institutions, and collective activities and interests.
- ❑ Impoverished. An unacceptably high number of people in the society are living below the poverty line.
- ❑ Development. The process of expanding an economy by investing in growth, with the side benefit of creating new jobs.

Perhaps the first question might be, "Are we really an impoverished society at this time in the United States?" For the country as a whole, that might be an exaggeration, but there are certainly areas within the country that you would designate as being impoverished.

Likewise, when you have underemployment in the vicinity of 15%, that is a significant number of people that, based on their income level, are living below the poverty line, so let's call it an impoverished society.

For those living the good life it might be hard to accept such a description of segments of our society. I recommend you slow down and take a look around you.[19] For more concrete evidence, examine where your tax dollars are going, with the large increases in unemployment benefits, the food stamp program and the Medicaid program, this at a time when the national debt is going out of sight.

The judgment that we are impoverished may be harsh, but again, look at the publicized figures with respect to unemployment. Currently, the federal government is reporting an unemployment rate of about 8%. That rate reflects the percentage of the normally working population that is actively looking for work, and does not include those who are no longer looking for work based on starting part-time work, frustration, age, or other factors. If we include these others, then the underemployment rate in the country is closer to 15% and if we look at isolated segments of the population, such as young black men we find extremely high underemployment rates that might lead us to conclude that, in fact, we are an impoverished society.

What's Wrong with Some Level of Poverty?

So we're setting out our second goal here of trying to eliminate poverty. Why is this so important? Wouldn't it be reasonable to assume that some percentage of our society could be living in poverty, and yet the country would be

---

[19] Once again, in 2012 we had about 15.5% of our population living in poverty, according to Associated Press surveys. That equates to about 46 million people.

functioning quite well? I submit that poverty, even at the level that is occurring in this country, is very significant in terms of the well being of the country. Consider these factors.

❑ <u>Hunger.</u> Do we really want people to be living in hunger in this country with our advanced civilization, and our somewhat extravagant lifestyle for many? It would seem to be a fairly straightforward conclusion that we do not want to have any significant number of the population living in hunger. Our goal should be to be sure they have the opportunity to get out of poverty. That's called employment opportunity.

❑ <u>Crime.</u> Some areas of the country have been hit with very high crime rates during this economic downturn. It should be obvious that unemployment plays a significant role in contributing to an environment conducive to crime.

I read recently where an author talked of living in a "company town" wherein the young people growing up were expecting to be educated and to be able to work for the company. This gave them a secure feeling of the future and assurance of a reasonable style of living.

Compare that then, to a city such as Stockton, California, where the underemployment rate is above 18% and ask yourself, "What do the young people here have to look forward to in terms of employment and the opportunity to enjoy a reasonable style of living?" I believe the coupling between under-employment and crime is very strong. Put another way, why would an individual that is earning a Living

Wage, and enjoying a reasonably comfortable lifestyle, decide to undertake criminal activity with the attendant high risk of being caught?

❑ <u>Class Warfare.</u> In the current environment some would say that we are witnessing class warfare between the haves and have-nots. This might be an exaggeration, but clearly it is not comfortable to see the middle class and above enjoying one lifestyle while the underemployed encounter an entirely different lifestyle. Not to say that we need to redistribute wealth. On the contrary, we need to provide employment opportunities that allow all of our citizens the chance to live a reasonable life. We can promise equal opportunity, but not equal outcomes.

In a later chapter, we will discuss the concept of the Living Wage and what that means to our population and to our economy. This is an extremely important concept that I believe the country should address. It's key to achieving expansion of the economy by increasing domestic markets.

Developing the Economy

Given that embarrassingly short list of reasons as to why poverty is bad, we can move on to discuss development of the economy so as to eliminate or at least greatly reduce unemployment. I use the term "Develop the Economy" with specific reference to the idea that increased private enterprise activity is the primary means by which we can accomplish increased employment. Private enterprise activity will occur in response to market demand.

The best chance we have for increasing economic activity initially is to encourage development in areas where the market demand may already exist. This increased activity, which will employ additional people, then creates additional market demand.[20] Further development can then respond to this demand. As I will discuss later there other areas that must be looked at if we are to continue to increase market demand. These include imports and the effect of outsourcing of jobs to overseas firms.

Financial resources must be available if economic development is to occur. Also, government regulations must encourage development, not hinder development. These two factors are the beginning of a long list of actions that can be taken to encourage economic development. While the issue is complex, the following actions can be taken. More details are provided in subsequent chapters in this book.

- ❏ Improve the atmosphere for private investment. Set up incentives and regulations that are in place for the longer-term and allow visibility, on the part of the potential investor, into the stability of these regulations and incentives.
- ❏ Reasonable tax rates. Implement tax rates that are consistent with encouraging private enterprise to invest in the development of our economy and that

---

[20] Some would define "Develop the Economy" as an exercise conducted by the Federal Government, providing stimulus funds, etc. I use the term strictly as the process of investing in private enterprise. Through such investment, companies are started/expanded in response to market demands. The underlying economy then undergoes growth, which can be measured by increases in the GDP.

allow small business people the resources to expand their businesses.

- ❑ <u>Reduce restrictions on development of natural resources.</u> Reduce government restrictions on development of natural resources, such as are involved in oil and natural gas exploration, development and production
- ❑ <u>Living Wage.</u> Encourage the payment of a Living Wage to full-time employees engaged in long-term work activities.
- ❑ <u>Foreign outsourcing.</u> Reduce foreign outsourcing through the establishment of incentives and public pressure.
- ❑ <u>Low wage imports.</u> Reduce low wage imports that compete unfairly with products manufactured in the United States.
- ❑ <u>Environmental protection</u>. Begin to strike a better balance with environmental protection goals in the interest of reducing unemployment in the short-term.
- ❑ <u>Global warming.</u> Strike a balance with man-made global warming goals while developing the economy.

In general, in a free market economy, economic development will occur where there is market demand and investors can perceive a return on their investment for the degree of risk taken. So, a simplified approach to determining actions that might be taken is to judge them based on those two criteria.

Typically in our economy there are always areas of market demand that are not being met. Usually these occur because there are some regulations or other limitations that delay or prevent development. These are obvious first targets for development because they offer the opportunity to invest in a shorter period of time. In the list of actions that can conceptually be taken, some can be implemented immediately and others will take major changes in the way we operate, in particular with respect to imports and exports.

Private Enterprise vs. Government Stimulus

The development of the economy by private enterprise has the advantage of providing employment opportunities, and those employment opportunities in turn, provide tax revenue for the government. It therefore seems reasonable to place economic development by private enterprise ahead of government stimulus spending since government stimulus spending typically can provide a short-term stimulus but not long-term employment.

The short list provided above barely scratches the surface with respect to actions that can and should be taken to develop the economy and thus create new jobs. An important aspect of this process is the recognition that the task is extensive, requiring many changes and improvements to our system.

A frustrating part of the equation, I'm sure, is that it will take time for development to occur once barriers to the creation of new and/or expanded businesses are lowered.[21] Increasing economic growth by development in the private

---

[21] One needs to understand that economic recovery is not a matter of just fixing one problem, but involves addressing the many problems that have been created by policies and regulations put into place over many years. This further complicates the task of exercising patience.

sector requires patience and understanding that in the long run this will produce a vital economy with much lower unemployment. There is no single magic bullet that will cure the unemployment problem.

Local Government Decline in Jobs

One of the side effects of the economic decline of the past few years has been the decline in revenues for local governments. This has resulted in significant layoffs as these governments strive to balance their budgets. In extreme cases, cities have been forced to file for bankruptcy.

There is a temptation on the part of the federal government to grant funds to these local entities to keep employment up. The problem occurs when the grant funding ends and the revenues have still not been restored.

It would seem logical that we should focus on developing the economy so that revenues to the local governments return to normal levels, thus allowing them to re-hire as needed.

Who are the Unemployed?

The above discussion applies in general to the problem of developing the economy. We need, however, to be aware of a problem in the mix of the unemployed. Recent data shows that the recovery to date for those with a college degree has been much better than those with a high school degree. So, when we are talking recovery, we need to be sure we are coming up with the right kind of jobs. I say this not from the detail level, but from the overall point of view.

I discussed earlier the housing bubble and subsequent burst that thrust a lot of people out of work. The follow-on financial collapse thrust more people out of work. The first to go were the construction workers, and many tend to not have college degrees. The subsequent layoffs affected everyone.

The data shows that in the comeback, the college-educated are in better shape. The construction people have generally not found work since new housing construction is still pretty much in the tank.

The net result is a situation wherein we have a much higher rate of unemployment for those with just high school education. We want to solve the unemployment problem so we better be aware of this lack of balance in the unemployed workforce. We cannot expect the housing construction industry to absorb all these people. The housing crisis is still being felt and, as I mentioned, the housing construction bubble employed an abnormal number of people before the bust, so we will still have a balance problem, even when housing construction gets back to normal.

All this suggests that in order to significantly reduce the underemployment rate in this recovery, we need to pay attention to the type of employment opportunities we are creating. Otherwise, we will decide that out problem must just be in education – in this global economy we need better education. I believe it is better to understand the problem up front, and work to solve it now, instead of waiting for a more effective educational system. And if we did decide the education is at fault and the solution is to correct it, what are all these currently unemployed folks supposed to do? More on this when we get to Foreign Outsourcing.

9...Private Sector Investment

In pursuing the concept of reducing unemployment by development of the economy we are looking to private enterprise to be the main provider of new jobs. So now we need to look at the motivating factors, the conditions necessary by which private enterprise will make the investments necessary to expand the economy and thus provide more jobs.

The Loss of Jobs

First I think it's worthwhile to look at some of the factors that have led to the current position of the United States with respect to unemployment. It is my opinion that this problem has been developing for a number of years. In fact, over the past 50 years there has been an increasing amount of import/export imbalance. It's most obvious when considering the automobile industry wherein Japanese automakers began selling their products in the U.S. in the 1960s. Over the following 34 years they established a quality of cars that allowed them to effectively compete with automakers in the United States. The net result of that, of course, was the loss of jobs in the U.S. The key to the success of Japan was the existence of relatively low labor costs and the realization that the products had to be of high quality. The same can be said for products that subsequently came from South Korea and now more recently from China. Those countries recognized that the keys to success in exporting to the U.S. involve quality and low costs.[22]

Should you disagree that the import/export balance has shifted dramatically I suggest a visit to a Home Depot or Lowe's home improvement center to conduct an examination of the country of origin of the products sold by these stores. They are selling two types of imported products in their stores. First are the true imports of products that are not now nor have they ever been made in the United States. Examples of these articles would be Persian rugs, native products etc.

The second type of product, and one that is becoming the prevalent type is that which is made in China, or other countries, to the specifications and design of companies located in the United States. For example inspect a dishwasher that is offered for sale by General Electric in this country and you will find that the product is, in fact being made in South Korea. This occurs because of the availability of low-cost labor in these countries and because the manufacturers are able to provide high quality.

The Housing Bubble

So what has happened is that American businesses, in order to be profitable and competitive, turn to outsourcing the manufacturing of their products and in some cases,

---

[22] A note of caution. Import/export is a two-way proposition. The U.S. and its trading partners have been very successful in some of their free trade agreements, resulting in healthy exports as well as imports.

services to foreign countries. This has been going on, as I stated previously, for at least 50 years. But, you might say, "In recent times how were we able to achieve the relatively low unemployment rates prevalent during the Clinton and Bush administrations with all this outsourcing occurring?"

I believe one can make a good case that the technology bubble and the housing bubble masked the problem to a great extent. The housing bubble caused homes prices to increase dramatically and created huge market demand. This was brought on by a lower cost of money (interest rates for borrowing) and the encouragement of politicians to have the banks finance mortgages for as many people as possible. When this occurred the economy benefited in a number of ways. Certainly the whole construction boom employed millions of individuals, most earning Living Wages.

This in turn increased the demand for products and services in the marketplace. A second factor occurred as follows. As the prices of homes increased homeowners were able to sell at a significant profit and again funds were available that caused the market demand to increase. When the housing bubble finally burst there were a number of factors that put us into the high unemployment condition, including the following.

❑ Falling prices put homes on the market at selling prices below the cost to construct. This situation clearly puts a damper on new home construction.

❑ New home construction plummeted, putting millions out of work

❑ Lower prices resulted in mortgages that were upside down, forcing foreclosures

❑ Lost jobs forced foreclosure

- ❏ A lingering problem was created. Foreclosed homeowners will likely be out of the market for 7 years or more as they re-establish their credit rating.

Our "Zero Defect" Society

Another very strong factor limiting the creation of jobs is government over-regulation. Our country has had the habit, in recent years, of expecting to see corrective action taken whenever a significant problem occurs. For example, in the Exxon accounting debacle the legislature and president reacted by putting in place the Sarbanes-Oxley Act. So here we had a company that was employing some accounting practices that were outside the realm of normal, and that eventually caused a collapse in the value of the company. The government then decided that they needed to put in new regulations to prevent such occurrences in the future.

The net effect of the action by the government was to create a very expensive and cumbersome accounting system for public companies, laid over that which already existed. This has had the side effect of discouraging private companies from going public because of the costs that must be incurred in implementing Sarbanes-Oxley. Without the mechanism for going public the venture capitalist has difficulty in seeing how he/she is going to realize liquidity for his/her investment. So, this is a case of the government putting on more regulations on the industry because of one company's errors. It results in penalties for all companies and a dampening of the investment market. So much for the zero defect society.

The flip side of this equation concerns public companies that are moving towards going private, again because of

Sarbanes-Oxley. There are a number of them that have done so, giving credence to the negative effects of Sarbanes-Oxley.[23]

In general there is a trend in our society to be more and more sophisticated with respect to our regulations. If you look at the history of the country you will find that each year there are new regulations that come into effect that are well intentioned but place more and more burden on private enterprise.

For example the regulations that that were included in the American Disabilities Act are laudable in making public facilities available to the handicapped, but they impose a sometimes significant and unrealistic burden on private enterprise. Once these regulations are put into place the laws are written such that the government entities enforcing the laws are generally not flexible. This overall philosophy of doing things exactly right or we won't approve it adds additional burden to the individual trying to run a profitable, growing company.

Another set of regulations concerning the environment has had a similar effect. Again the regulations were intended to protect the environment, which is a worthwhile cause. However the implementation of the regulations places a burden on those that would develop the economy and this burden, while originally intended to be well defined, has become a never-ending process.

---

[23] The cost of implementing the policies of Sarbanes-Oxley must be covered by the affected companies, and these costs are not insignificant. This, in turn, leads to a further reduction in their ability to compete in the global economy.

For example if one is to develop a subdivision in a community an environmental impact report is typically required in most states. The rules surrounding environmental impact reports are very specific with respect to notices to the public and how responses from the public and other entities should be handled. In practice it turns out that regulations regarding this process are often ignored for what appear to be, on the surface, very good reasons.

The process allows for a specific comment period, after which the issue is to be closed for further comment. In practice what often happens is that individuals or organizations either do not get notified of the environmental impact report or are not timely in their filing of responses. Since the responses often are the subject of serious consideration, the entire process gets delayed.

In a time of high unemployment such as we are encountering in 2012 it would make sense to follow the original regulations to the letter of the law, and perhaps even place new regulations which would allow one to expedite (fast track) these approval cycles so that development (be it housing or commercial) can move ahead. This is a benefit to society in that it creates new jobs, yet still provides for the intent of the environmental protection acts.

The bottom line of all of these considerations is this. We need to have a business environment in the United States that encourages investment in projects that will provide additional employment. We need to change the current regulatory environment and tip the balance more in favor of development rather than endless protections. Only by this process will we see investment that will allow us to development the economy and reduce unemployment.

10...Infrastructure and Energy

Infrastructure Needs

In the U.S. our government is heavily involved in the development of infrastructure and energy systems. Of the two, the infrastructure is clearly an important role for the government. People at the local, county, city, state or federal level governments are typically responsible for the building of highways and utilities. It is also true that in the year 2012 some of our infrastructure around the country is in need of update.

I would suggest that the proper way for the government to execute improvements to the infrastructure is through careful planning and long-term establishment of budgets and goals. When trying to use the improvement of infrastructure as a means of reducing unemployment we end up with relatively short-term projects that provide temporary employment, and, if executed before economic growth is restored, cause the debt of the government agency to increase.

Politicians are often anxious to get funds allocated for projects in their districts. Many times these projects involve infrastructure. In times of economic hardship, it would seem to be appropriate to focus on development of the economy to reduce unemployment and achieve the attendant increase in tax resources, for example, that can then be used to support infrastructure improvements.

Energy Sources

On the energy front, we have a significant opportunity to reduce underemployment. There are many energy-related projects that can be undertaken that provide added capacity for our country. The world demand for energy is increasing as China and India become modernized. Therefore, the world supply of oil is under pressure and oil prices are relatively high. We have the opportunity to move towards foreign oil independence by further development of our own natural resources.

Let's first take the example of the BP oil spill in the Gulf of Mexico region. Here again is an example of government and public reaction to a problem that did not necessarily come about for lack of regulations. The accident and resulting oil spill came about because of a failure of a piece of equipment and the inappropriate action by those operating a drill rig during the failure. The government's reaction, however, was to demand that we put into place stronger preventive measures and licensing procedures so that this type of accident "will not happen again." The result of that response has included an initial moratorium on development of oil fields in the area and then, once the moratorium ended, increased time delays for obtaining new permits.

All combined, these actions have resulted in the loss of a significant number of jobs relating to work in the Gulf of Mexico and they have reduced the supply of oil produced in the United States.

There are instances where improvements in laws and regulations should be made based on what we've learned from our day-to-day experiences. As stated, our country generally tends to want to react to accidents and/or improper actions by passing new laws and regulations. The example above is only one of many we've seen the past few years. Most of them have contributed to the problem of underemployment.

The BP oil spill is not unique in terms of our government putting into place policies and regulations that limit oil production in this country. Our country has debated at length over the wisdom of developing the oil fields adjacent to the Artic National Wildlife Refuge (ANWR) in the Northern Slopes of Alaska. Worries about the environment have precluded development of an extensive oil field that would increase domestic production of oil and have a stabilizing effect on the price of oil.

I suggest that we should look more closely at developing the North Slope, using environmentally responsible methods. Some have said that such development will have no impact on the price of oil because of the length of time that it takes to get the wells into production. I suggest that what appears to be a long-term solution now becomes a short-term solution six years from now when we are still trying to address foreign oil dependency and unemployment problems.

The same argument can be made for development of coastal oilfields wherein the government has severely restricted issuance of permits for off shore oil exploration and production.

In spite of these restrictions we read that new oilfield developments are increasing in recent years, primarily because of activity on private land. The trend is in the right direction and can be further enhanced by opening up more development on federal lands.

In recent years we have seen success in extracting oil and natural gas from previously inaccessible formations using hydraulic fracturing methods (fracking). This is proving to be a very valuable capability that promises further progress in achieving foreign oil independence. This is a significant opportunity for the country, but is becoming the subject of debate by environmentalists. Here we go again!

Energy Goals

This leads us into a discussion of what our goals should be with respect to energy production. Energy plays an important role in the process of reaching our goal of reducing unemployment. In particular, the use of electrical energy is tied tightly to the advancement of a society. The generation of electricity throughout the world has evolved from hydro-electric to coal and oil powered plants to the use of natural gas, nuclear power, wind power and solar power.

There's clearly a very concerted global effort to have all countries in the world reduce hydrocarbon emissions to prevent man-made global warming. Well, you can argue, and many will, about the scientific veracity of the man-made global warming argument. I suggest that the argument is a mute point. The fact is, at the moment our lack of foreign oil independence is causing economic difficulties in our country. We need to continue to develop our natural resources of oil, and natural gas. This will give us a strong baseline from which we can move towards hydrocarbon free energy generation.

Following that thread, we should discuss the current moves towards "hydrocarbon free" energy sources. We have major movements in this country pushing towards developing wind and solar resources for the production of electrical energy. We also have an effort underway to utilize corn to produce ethanol as a means of reducing our consumption of oil. In general these efforts lead toward the production of electrical energy or fuel with minimal discharge of hydrocarbons to the atmosphere (with the exception of ethanol). However, the amount of energy produced is relatively small compared to the total consumption in our country.[24]

In striking a decision on what alternate sources of energy should be pursued, it's important to construct a model of how the economy and the energy markets will behave should the efforts become successful.

In the case of ethanol from corn we, after the fact, are learning that the net effect of producing ethanol from corn has had minor impact on the energy market, but has had a major impact on the cost of food. Corn, is a food staple in many countries.[25] For example, it turns out that corn is a major staple in the diet of the people of Nicaragua, and with the high percentage of unemployment and underemployment

---

[24] These efforts, to try to force movement away from oil, are often premature. History has shown that in the end, economics will sort out which technologies are best. We are better off supporting research into various alternatives and then letting the market determine which survive.

[25] We really need to put politics aside and think through the damage we are creating by messing with the food chain. Seriously folks, we are messing with people's lives here.

in Nicaragua, the government has found it necessary to subsidize the price of corn so that the poor do not starve.

I believe that we should focus our research and development efforts on nuclear energy in parallel with all the other efforts. There are new developments in the nuclear electrical generation field that look very promising and involve the production of nuclear power plants that are intrinsically much safer than those previously deployed. Concepts such as the General Electric Hitachi Prism power plant should be further explored and developed as that type of plant is able to rely on passive control of the radioactive reaction (safer) and conceptually will be able to burn fuel that has been depleted in the current generation nuclear power plants (use of nuclear waste). There's no guarantee that this or any other specific idea will be the best approach. Only the application of research and development and pilot production will bear out the feasibility of each idea.

The public is anxious regarding the safety aspects of the generation of electricity. We've had problems occasionally with the nuclear power plants of the current generation design. The most recent problem occurred in Japan and was an extremely serious problem. But technology has advanced since those power plants were designed and we should not let those accidents deter us from exploring the feasibility of building safer, more reliable nuclear power plants.

In the nuclear power plant industry we have learned that training of the operators and reliability of the equipment are extremely important. From this we've learned that we should design these power plants to a set of standards. Utilizing these standards, we can then learn from operation of other power plants. In other words, should one power plant have a maintenance problem, all other plants of the same design can benefit from the experience. Likewise, operators can be trained to operate these plants as an industry discipline, a fact that should result in safer operation.

The Automobile

Since we've mentioned the subject of man-made global warming and the general public concern over this, the next logical area of exploration is perhaps the automobile. In recent years we've seen a very strong push towards battery powered electric autos or hybrid versions using a gas engine to recharge the batteries. The driving force for such changes centers on the desire to eliminate hydrocarbon emissions from gasoline powered autos. The concept is an old concept and suffers from a couple of problems.

The first and most important problem is that the battery needs to be recharged after each use. That means utilizing power from the electrical grid to charge the batteries. If the electricity was generated by a power plant with hydrocarbon emissions such as that encountered in coal-fired power plants, natural gas power plants and oil-fired power plants, then we are, in fact, generating hydrocarbons into the atmosphere when recharging the batteries. To therefore say that the batteries are a pollution-free source of energy is a fallacy.

This an area where we need the government and specifically the EPA to get real in terms of what's happening when we utilize an all-electric or hybrid gas-electric car. The fact is that energy in the form of electrical energy is being generated somewhere to charge the batteries. When you look at the total hydrocarbon emissions associated with the hybrid car, to include manufacturing of the car and the batteries, it's very doubtful that you could consider these vehicles to be non-hydrocarbon emitting vehicles.

Transportable Energy Sources

The problem boils down to this. We need a transportable form of energy that is not hydrocarbon emitting in order to power our automobiles. Gasoline qualifies as a transportable form of energy but in the process of generating the energy to power the car, hydrocarbons are emitted. Therefore it does not qualify. The battery itself does not emit hydrocarbons while it's being used to power the cars but the electricity used to charge the batteries very likely comes from a carbon dioxide emitting source. The same may be said for the hybrid car that causes hydrocarbon release during the charging cycle and hydrocarbon release from the gas engine if the batteries are recharged in transit.

There is one form of transportable energy that qualifies for the above restriction, and that is hydrogen as it is used to power a fuel cell. Experimental vehicles are in use in various cities around the country, with the fuel cell cars having been manufactured by the automobile manufacturers on an experimental basis. They utilize the fuel cell powered by hydrogen. The fuel cell generates electricity and the process produces water as a byproduct, with no hydrocarbon emissions.

The concept is not without some problems, including the current cost to manufacture and the driving range achievable with current methods of storing the hydrogen. There is of course the need to generate the hydrogen and this requires the expenditure of energy. It is possible to produce the hydrogen in a process using natural gas and it is also possible to produce the hydrogen using electrolysis of water. Since our goal is to not utilize fossil fuels this type of transportation would be successful if we envisioned nuclear or other non-polluting power as a source of energy to create the hydrogen from water.

Of course, having gone through that explanation. You may readily conclude that batteries by themselves are a form of transportable energy. Absent hydrocarbon emissions, and provided again that they are charged from a nuclear power source (or other non-hydrocarbon emitting source) these are a legitimate solution to the problem. The difficulty in the solution lies in the cost and process of manufacturing the batteries and the limited range that current battery technology provides. Most electric automobiles envisioned in the current time frame have rather severe limitations to their driving range on a single charge. This really limits the usefulness of these cars and the solution is not a good fit to the way our country is laid out in terms of cities, urban areas and the resulting need for personal transportation.[26]

In Summary

We need good long-term planning in our country regarding improvements that should be made to our infrastructure. Only by planning ahead will we plan the budgets required to support such activities.

---

[26] Trying to change the structure of our cities and urban areas will be a lot more expensive and disruptive to our country than quietly pursuing solutions to the transportable energy problem that will allow us to continue to utilize the automobile for transportation.

In the energy area, we need to gain independence from foreign oil. With about half of our oil purchases being made from foreign countries, we have a balance of trade problem. Such purchases are draining funds from our country that might otherwise contribute to the development of our economy.

We need to be more careful in planning alternate energy sources and what side effects they may have, such as has happened with corn prices.

We need to be realistic in our quest for transportable energy sources for automobiles, sources that do not emit hydrocarbon by-products, either on the road or at power plants that provide the power to achieve transportable energy.

In the end, we need to look more closely at nuclear power as a source of clean energy. Specifically, we should be supporting research and development into new generation nuclear power plants that are designed to be inherently safer.

It will take time to develop the technologies needed to slow down and eventually replace the use of hydrocarbon emitting energy sources. The problem is one of both economics and technology. In the meantime, we should be exploiting our natural resources to achieve independence from foreign oil.

11... A Living Wage Benefit

The Concept

In our list of actions that can be taken to develop the economy we slipped in the concept of paying a Living Wage to employees. This is a very important aspect in the development of an impoverished society. While many may associate the concept with the modern trends concerning social justice, I am presenting the concept as an important method of lifting people out of poverty by expanding markets.

The concept of paying a Living Wage is not new. It's a method of compensation to employees that allows the employee some form of homeownership/rental and covers basic needs for transportation, healthcare, clothing, nutrition, social life, recreation and some form of retirement for the future. Calculation of a Living Wage is sensitive to the costs associated with the area in which the individual lives and is sensitive to marital status, size of family, and other factors.

The concept of a Living Wage was initially explored by Pope Leo the 13th in 1891 when he published the papal bull entitled "Rerum Novarum." In this writing the Pope was concerned about the conflict between capitalism and socialism. He concluded that the property ownership aspects of capitalism are important to human nature but also concluded that individuals have a right to earn a Living Wage when working for others.

To quote Pope Leo:

"Let the working man and the employer make free agreements, and in particular let them agree freely as to the wages; nevertheless, there underlies a dictate of natural justice more imperious and ancient than any bargain between man and man, namely, that wages ought not to be insufficient to support a frugal and well-behaved wage-earner. If through necessity or fear of a worse evil the workman accepts harder conditions because an employer or contractor will afford him no better, he is made the victim of force and injustice."

The Pope showed remarkable insight into the relationship between a person and his/her employer. While I agree with the social justice aspect of the Living Wage concept, I think an equally powerful argument centers on the effect of the Living Wage in the marketplace.

As previously stated there are currently a number of organizations in the U.S. promoting the concept of employment with a Living Wage.[27] These organizations mostly justify the payment of a Living Wage as a matter of social justice. The arguments for a Living Wage made by these organizations are certainly justified, but I would make the argument that the economic benefit of paying Living Wages is an important part of recovery from our current environment as we develop the economy.

---

[27] According to the Wikipedia website, there are seven prominent organizations pursuing the living wage goal. The total effort is most likely much larger.

The Importance of the Concept

With all the current talk about interest rates, taxation rates, stimulus packages, and other means of trying to accomplish the creation of new jobs, you may wonder why I would argue that the Living Wage is such an important aspect of solving the unemployment problem. While our unemployment problem is not nearly as severe as that existing in Nicaragua, for example, that country's under-employment problem illustrates well how one might attack the problem utilizing Living Wages.

With more than 50% underemployment in Nicaragua, the country presents a clearly defined set of circumstances under which underemployment must be reduced. There are a number of characteristics that define the problem, and at the same time point towards a solution that includes consideration of implementation of Living Wages. For example, in that country, a worker constructing a very modest middle-class home cannot afford to purchase that home. Schoolteachers cannot afford to purchase the most basic of homes.

Doubling the minimum wage that is in place in Nicaragua does not solve the problem. The country does have a serious problem though, that opens the way towards a partial solution to the underemployment. This problem is a lack of housing, estimated to be in the order of 500,000 units in a country with a population of approximately 6,000,000 people. Calculations show that constructing homes, when the workers are paid a Living Wage, results in a situation wherein the workers are the market for the homes.

It is relatively easy, in this case, to see that paying Living Wages to the workers constructing the homes creates a good part of the market for the homes. In our complex society it is more difficult to readily identify this relationship between Living Wages and the creation of a market need. Suffice to say, the payment of Living Wages to those previously trapped in poverty opens up new markets for goods and services for all.

Here's a question for you to ponder. "In a free market capitalistic economy is it intrinsically necessary to have companies survive off the backs of low-paid workers?" Historically this has been a characteristic of many economies. The most extreme example, of course, is the use of slavery. But beyond that we have seen many examples of companies succeeding based on utilizing low-cost labor. We see it today in our farming industry where, by the nature of the seasonal work, the farm workers are paid a relatively low wage. From the free market viewpoint we don't want to legislate or force implementation of Living Wages, as that would severely restrict economic activity. We can however set as a goal the gradual implementation of the Living Wage concept.

Market Leverage

On the national front there is ongoing debate about how to increase employment, with a lot of attention being paid to income tax rates, borrowing rates, and the offering of economic incentives to small businesses. However none of these techniques can be fully effective if market demand is not present. I argued earlier that the best chance jumpstarting the economy in terms of increasing employment is to attack areas where market demand already exists. Development in these areas will increase employment. The increased employment will, in turn, create an increased market for goods and services if the employees are paid Living Wages. It's easy to show in the previously discussed Nicaragua case that if the construction employees were paid Living Wages they would be able to afford the homes they are building. This would expand the economy and the markets for other goods and services.[28]

Setting Priorities

This Living Wage concept has ramifications in a number of different areas. In developing countries, for example, where the standard of living is lower and low-cost labor is more readily available, production of imports to the United States results in lower product costs than can be achieved by personnel working in this country. This is especially true when employees in this country are being paid Living Wages. In a sense this represents a dilemma. Do we want to participate in trying to uplift the economy of developing countries at the expense of our own economy or do we prefer to have protection from these imports so that the employees in this country can earn Living Wages.

Likewise in this country, the Living Wage concept might preclude making certain products for export, depriving folks of at least some wages, even if below the poverty rate. Aren't folks better off with something, rather than nothing?

I suggest that this country needs to place a higher priority on setting policies and regulations that allow employers in the

---

[28] A recent article was posted on foreignpolicy.com entitled "Lions on the Move." It describes the success Africa has had in creating employment by investing in their economy. They describe the importance of enlarging the "consuming class" wherein people can direct more than half of their income to things other than shelter and food.

United States to, for the most part, pay Living Wages to their employees. On the other hand I do not suggest that the payment of Living Wages by private enterprise employers be made mandatory. If that were to occur the net result would be a decrease in employment, as it would rule out the hiring of unskilled workers that could receive on-the-job training. It would rule out the hiring of youth or perhaps those working part-time, working their way through school, and it would preclude hiring with lower level wages where the company is willing to train the individual to become fully productive employees with the required skill sets. The same problem occurs when considering raising the minimum wage within the country and we've devoted a chapter to the discussion of that problem.

So, I argue that Living Wages and the payment thereof in our society are an important aspect in the development of an impoverished society. I can think of many examples where the payment of wages that leave a person living in poverty produce the wrong effect. Consider a disadvantaged person living in a distressed area and in his own mind trying to decide whether to sell drugs or to get a job. If he gets a job that results in his total wages being below the poverty line his expectations are greatly diminished and he is more likely to decide to sell drugs.

A Job or a Career?

There was recently a report on cable television, wherein the reporter interviewed people who were drawing unemployment checks. One of the individuals interviewed, when asked if he was looking for a job, stated, "No, he was not looking for a job, he was looking for career." At the time the comment seemed funny to the reporter. I thought about what this gentleman was really trying to say. I think he was trying to say that he's not looking for a low-paying job that will keep him living in poverty. He's looking for a job that allows him to state that he has a career, that he earns a Living Wage and that he can support himself and his family in a reasonable way.

While you might view the foregoing argument as one of implementing social justice, I believe that this is one case where we're fortunate to have a common motivation for paying a Living Wage. The technique implements social justice, and equally, if not more importantly, in the long term increases the market for goods and services that contribute to acceleration in the job growth of the economy.[29]

Negative Impacts to be Mitigated

All in all this sounds great from the standpoint of the individual. There are those who will justifiably say that this upsets the economic model of many businesses. Farming for example involves seasonal employment and in the last century farmers normally brought individuals from lower cost-of-living areas such as Mexico into this country to carry out farm labor tasks.

---

[29] While I believe strongly in social justice, pursuit of the Living Wage on that basis alone leads to government enforcement by fiat. This can be destructive to the free enterprise system. Pursuit of the Living Wage as an economic advantage in pursuing economic recovery fits well within the free enterprise system, yet accomplishes the social justice goal. Our elected officials need to understand the immense value in keeping and expanding the "consuming class."

Needless to say it will be difficult to implement the Living Wage concept for farm workers. Implementation of the Living Wage concept in farming is going to mean that prices for food may have to increase some amount to compensate for the increased wages. This in turn places the farmer at an economic disadvantage with respect to low-cost imports and raises the possibility again that some policies may need to be set in place to protect local businesses from products that are produced by those living in low standard of living countries.

Another area that would be if impacted with the introduction of Living Wages is the fast food industry, notorious for paying low wages and few benefits. The Living Wage implementation will obviously cause the cost of fast foods to increase.

There are those that have argued that the poor are one of the main consumers of fast food (because of the low cost) and that by implementing the Living Wage concept in this industry we would increase the prices of food to the poor. I suggest that the poor in this case include those who are working in the fast food industry and that if they're being paid minimum wages they are likely living below the poverty line. I would rather see a movement to have Living Wages be paid to these individuals so that they, as well as everyone else, can afford the fast food items. The price increases to middle class and above customers will likely not be bothersome.

When you think about this from the social viewpoint you have to ask the question, "Is it fair for the middle class and above to be consuming fast food at a bargain prices because the workers in that industry are living in poverty. That makes no sense from the social justice viewpoint. I would suggest that the general public, i.e. the voter, has the capability to see this implementation through by exercising their freedom as to where they work, and by encouraging implementation based on where they buy their fast food. (No, not a boycott, but a freedom to choose where to eat.)   Another note of caution: many of the part time and entry-level jobs provided by fast food restaurants are extremely valuable to young people. They provide an entry point into the job market, and they often provide financial support for students. One must be careful to not destroy these jobs.

Finally, there are those that will say that this is just another income re-distribution scheme. "You are effectively suggesting in your economic model that everyone pay a little more for goods and services so that the wages of low end workers can be raised to Living Wages. That's income re-distribution."

OK, then let's consider professional athletes. They are paid huge salaries, upwards of millions per year for their services. In their economic model, the teams derive their revenue from gate receipts and TV advertising. Companies that advertise raise their prices to cover their advertising budget. So, the average Joe is paying more for goods and services provided by those who advertise (and buying tickets to the games) so that the sports figures can be paid their millions. That's income re-distribution!

No disrespect, but I like the Living Wage model better.

Implementation

So, in the preceding we laid out some of the difficult aspects of implementing Living Wage concepts in this country. That brings us to the point of how one can accomplish this goal without causing economic chaos for those businesses that currently pay minimum wages instead of Living Wages. As I stated before I would suggest that one should not make payment of Living Wages a hard and fast law. That approach will cause economic chaos.

In order to more clearly define the concept proposed, I suggest that we should define the proposal as a "Living Wage Benefit." This more accurately defines the proposal as a benefit.

If we look at the history of other benefits that have been and/or are provided by businesses we find that benefits are provided mainly as a competitive tool to be used in their hiring practices. For example, a large percentage of businesses now offer healthcare insurance for their employees as a benefit. How did this come about?

It turns out that in the post-World War II era our economy was in a growth stage and businesses were hiring. The market for skilled workers was competitive, particularly, on the West Coast. Businesses began offering paid health insurance as an enticement to work for their companies. Once in place that benefit essentially became a standard in the industry and has remained to this day, absent consideration of the largely unknown effects of the new Affordable Care Act.[30]

---

[30] As of July 2012, 57% of small (<100 employees) and 89% of large (>500 employees) companies offered medical insurance. 50% of small and 86% of large companies offered retirement benefits, according to Government data. 99% of local and state governments offered medical and retirement benefits. Shall we guess the numbers for the Federal Government employees?

Another benefit to employees that is taken for granted concerns the allowing of time off for holidays on a paid basis. This benefit, that usually includes 12 to 15 paid holidays per year, has become a routine benefit for nearly all companies in the United States. While not emphasized, it is, in fact, a benefit that is expected on the part of all new hires. If it is not available, the company will have difficulty in attracting new employees.

From these experiences, I suggest that competition for employees is an effective way of seeing a gradual implementation of the Living Wage concept. With an excess supply of labor available at this time, the concept will be weak, but as the unemployment and underemployment figures come down there be more competition for the hiring of individuals. The Living Wage Benefit can then become a strong part of the competitive package that businesses can offer in order to successfully hire.

As previously stated, there are currently many groups in the United States that are promoting the concept of paying Living Wages. At least one of these suggests that initially the government should make up the difference between actual wages and Living Wages. This approach increases employee dependence on the federal government and sets up a conflict between the government and the company as to who pays what.

A more reasonable approach to the implementation of the Living Wage Benefit would be to phase in the concept as stated above. This approach would create less economic disruption on the companies, would allow young people the opportunity to work for lower wages for entry-level jobs, and would be consistent with free market competitive principles.

As the country recovers from the unemployment problem, hiring will become more and more competitive, and Living Wage Benefits will logically come into place. Public choice in buying products from companies can also influence the rate of adoption of Living Wage Benefits.[31]

Quantifying the Living Wage

Try doing a Goggle search on the words "Living Wage" and you will find that there are many ways to define a reasonable Living Wage. To begin with it clearly depends upon the cost-of-living in the area in which the employee resides. Therefore, a uniform Living Wage across the country makes no sense. Second, a Living Wage for a family depends upon the number of members in the family that are working. In other words, the Living Wage for a husband whose wife stays at home to look after the children would be much higher than his wage when both he and his wife are working. The definition then becomes a measure of one's individual circumstances. The Living Wage Benefit should be defined in simpler terms and not be defined by family size, etc. when we are trying to lift people out of poverty.

Another factor that influences the level of Living Wages concerns the nature of the job. In many companies there are career jobs and there are entry-level and perhaps temporary jobs. I'm suggesting that implementation of the Living Wage concept be done on a voluntary basis for that reason. One

---

[31] For many companies, this is a no-brainer. Their payroll structure is such that they can easily adopt the Living Wage Benefit. They are then in the position of being able to advertise this fact, and perhaps gain an advantage in hiring the best people.

does not want to inhibit a company from hiring unskilled labor to give these folks the opportunity to learn on the job and advance to career positions. Likewise, one wants to preserve the capability of the company to hire young people in the 18 to 25-year-old bracket.

Such factors illustrate the complexity of implementing the Living Wage Benefit. It suggests that private or public entities should undertake the task of determining Living Wage levels in their local areas. This would provide a basis by which companies can determine if they are in fact paying Living Wages to their employees.

The concept of paying Living Wages in the United States needs to be encouraged. One method of encouragement is to publicize the goals and to educate the population on the value of implementing the payment of Living Wages. We should encourage companies to advertise their willingness to pay Living Wages. As previously stated, if consumers of the company's products are aware of the pay standards of the company, they are in a position to decide whether or not to buy the company's products, with that knowledge being made a part of the decision. In other words, the public has the opportunity to vote with their purchasing power. Obviously, if a company must raise prices in order to implement a Living Wage policy, this places the consumer in the position of perhaps paying more for that company's products.

12...Housing Construction - a Way Out

When there is a Housing Shortage

By its nature, housing construction can be an excellent contributor to reducing unemployment. The housing construction industry has the advantage that it's usually not subjected to foreign outsourcing problems in that the construction workers usually reside in country. It represents an industry that can accommodate skilled and unskilled workers.

It's fairly straightforward to set up a mathematical model of housing construction. In such a model one can make assumptions with regard to the number of man-hours needed to build a home, the type of home that one would seek to build, and the costs of building materials and land associated with such construction.

I've run such a model for lower middle class homes on the assumption that there is a very large market for these homes, either as new or as replacements for existing homes in slums. It turns out that for reasonable numbers of construction workers required to build each home and assuming they are built in a lower-cost area where land values do not unreasonably distort the cost, a company that seeks to build 100 homes the first year, and then seeks to increase its production by 50% each year will employ enough workers that they themselves basically become the market for these new homes for the first five years.

This self-fulfilling market occurs because the employees are paid a Living Wage. At first thought you might conclude that the best way to provide housing for impoverished societies is to build the lowest cost homes possible using very low cost labor, so that low income people can afford to buy or rent the house. But it turns out that a better strategy is to pay employees Living Wages for construction of the housing, so that they are part of the potential market.

Financing

Were one to embark on such a building program, financing is critical. One basically needs to develop this home building project through financing of the construction of the homes. Since we are dealing with previously unemployed or underemployed individuals, we cannot assume that they are credit worthy to the point that they can purchase a home with bank financing. So, besides financing the construction of the homes, one needs a financing program for the homebuyers.[32]

A savings and loan type financial organization with a charter to provide rental, lease and lease with option to buy programs would allow these first-time home occupiers to develop a financial history and eventually have a credit rating

---

[32] Various sources indicate that in excess of 15 million foreclosures have occurred since 2006. This indicates a very large segment of would-be homeowners with a wounded credit rating, many of whom have the income to support a modest home purchase.

worthy of bank financing. The magnitude of funding required for such a development is not insignificant, but is key to developing an impoverished society by this method.

With the advent of construction companies that pay Living Wages to those building the homes, a portion of the population becomes part of the market for goods and services for the population in general. Thus, there is leverage on the wages paid to these employees, and they, in turn, will spend money for goods and services of a general nature. The idea of the impoverished building homes for the impoverished thus becomes the beginning of a society that is being lifted from poverty.

13...Minimum Wage

Ongoing Debate

Over the years there has been much discussion about the minimum wage laws at the federal, state and local level. There are those who see minimum wage laws as a means of being certain that employees receive a Living Wage. There are others who see minimum wage laws as being a negative factor in employment, actually causing reduced employment.

Historically minimum wages have been set well below the poverty level. As such, they protect entry-level employees. Minimum wage laws are continuously debated and rates are adjusted in the upward direction, but there's really been no resolution between the opposing viewpoints.[33]

Setting the minimum wages to high levels clearly can provide Living Wages to employees. The problem occurs in cases of part-time work, entry-level work, and employment of young people. High minimum wages also severely restrict the employment capabilities of the various employing entities. As discussed in Chapter 11 the issue is not whether

---

[33] As of the end of 2012, minimum wage rates, as set by the states, varied from a low of $5.15 per hour to a high of $9.04 per hour. The Federal rate was $7.25 per hour.

employees should be paid a Living Wage. That is clearly an admirable goal for full-time employees that are supporting themselves and their families.

Negative Consequences

More to the point, the issue is one of forcing employers to pay the higher minimum wages. This takes away flexibility on the part of the employer and severely restricts his or her ability to hire. Remember, the subject here is how to reduce unemployment. In the process of utilizing free market capitalism as the foundation of reducing unemployment, we need to keep in mind that we want as many employment opportunities as possible in this downside economy. Forcing high minimum wages can clearly result in fewer jobs.

A major impact of high minimum wages concerns entry-level employment, particularly when addressing the severe problems of underemployment in the 18 to 25 year old category. This is a critical time in a person's life when they need to experience successful work, as that lays the foundation for their future. While current levels of minimum wage are really set below the poverty level, we need to recognize that entry-level people (young people) often have shared living arrangements with parents or friends and are in a different position with respect to their financial needs in those early years. It is far better for them to have an employment opportunity, even if below Living Wage levels.

Another class to consider is part-time workers. In this case the individuals may not be seeking a career but looking for a way to supplement their income. Setting the minimum wage laws to require high minimum wages can restrict opportunities for these people.

Finally, I'm going to suggest that one method of reducing underemployment amongst those who are not fully qualified for their jobs is to encourage companies to hire people at these average minimum wage levels and train them, with incentives such as tax credits being provided by the government. This is one way to speed up the cycle of reducing unemployment, addressing the needs of those less educated or less experienced.

Keeping the Door Open

While politicians and unions press for higher minimum wages, I really believe that a less formal means of advancement to higher wages is a more appropriate model for our country, particularly for the situation in which we find ourselves. I know this is hard for some folks to agree with but I really believe that we need to keep the employment door open for young people and give them the chance to learn, on-the-job if necessary, and therefore to advance to the point where they too can achieve Living Wages.

14...Foreign Outsourcing

In recent years more and more companies are turning to foreign outsourcing for the manufacturing of their products. These companies often (but not always) design the products in the U.S., do foreign manufacturing, and then do worldwide marketing and selling. The net result is a dramatic shift of the manufacturing jobs to foreign countries.

I'll cover more on these lost jobs in Chapter 15. Meanwhile, just in case you are not convinced of the extent to which this has happened, please consider the following list of companies and products that are manufactured outside the United States. In fairness, I should list those who manufacture in the U.S., but in random sampling at local retailers, this is what I encountered.

Small Appliances.
- ❏ Keurig Coffee Maker – China
- ❏ Cuisinart Coffee Maker – China
- ❏ Mr. Coffee, Coffee Maker – China
- ❏ Hamilton Beach Brew Station – China

Tools.
- ❏ Kobalt Tools – China

- ❏ Dremel Tools – Mexico
- ❏ Skill Table Saw – China

Hardware Supplies.
- ❏ Velcro – U.S.A.
- ❏ Grip Rite Screws – Taiwan
- ❏ Grip Rite Nails – U.A.E.
- ❏ Hillman Screws
  - ✓ Taiwan
  - ✓ China
  - ✓ Canada
  - ✓ U.S.A.
  - ✓ Korea
- ❏ Brainerd Cabinet Knobs – China
- ❏ Kwikset Door Knobs – Mexico
- ❏ Schlage Locks – Mexico
- ❏ Baldwin Door Locks – Philippines

Home Decorations.
- ❏ Allen + Roth Mirrors - China

Clothing (by Manufacturer).
- ❏ Calvin Kline
  - ✓ Shirts – Indonesia
  - ✓ Slacks – Bangladesh
  - ✓ T-shirts – China
- ❏ Tommy Hilfiger
  - ✓ T-shirts – Cambodia
  - ✓ Jeans – Columbia
  - ✓ Shorts – Bangladesh

- ❏ Nautica
  - ✓ T-shirts – Vietnam
  - ✓ Swimsuits – Cambodia
  - ✓ Windbreakers – China
  - ✓ Shirts – Bangladesh
  - ✓ Jeans – Mexico
- ❏ La Coste
  - ✓ T-shirts – El Salvador
- ❏ Champion
  - ✓ T-shirts – Honduras
  - ✓ Vests – Honduras
- ❏ Adidas
  - ✓ Sweat Shirts – Indonesia
  - ✓ T-shirts – Cambodia
  - ✓ T-shirts – Honduras
  - ✓ Jackets – Indonesia
- ❏ Nike
  - ✓ Socks – U.S.A.
  - ✓ T-shirts – Mexico
  - ✓ Shorts – Thailand
  - ✓ T-shirts – Taiwan
- ❏ Alfani
  - ✓ Underwear - Pakistan
- ❏ Ralph Lauren
  - ✓ Shirts – India
  - ✓ Shorts – Vietnam
  - ✓ T-shirts – Vietnam
  - ✓ T-shirts – Mexico
  - ✓ Hats – China

- ❑ American Rag
  - ✓ Shirts – China
  - ✓ Jeans – Bangladesh
  - ✓ Shirts – Bangladesh
  - ✓ Jeans – Cambodia
- ❑ Jockey
  - ✓ T-shirts – Columbia
  - ✓ Boxers – Costa Rica
- ❑ Levi Strauss
  - ✓ Jeans – Bangladesh
  - ✓ Jeans – Mexico
  - ✓ Jeans – Egypt
  - ✓ Jeans – Columbia
- ❑ Kenneth Cole
  - ✓ Shirts – Thailand
- ❑ Calvin Kline
  - ✓ Underwear – Thailand
  - ✓ Women's Shoes - China
- ❑ Polo Ralph Loren
  - ✓ T-shirts – India
  - ✓ Briefs – China
- ❑ Hillfiger
  - ✓ Watches – China
- ❑ Reebok
  - ✓ Shoes – Vietnam
- ❑ DKNY
  - ✓ Women's Shoes – China

- ❑ Perry Ellis
  - ✓ Shirts – Indonesia

- ❑ Van Heusen
  - ✓ Shirts – Indonesia
- ❑ Eddie Bauer
  - ✓ Shirts – Madagascar
  - ✓ Shirts – Hong Kong
- ❑ Roundtree & York
  - ✓ Shirts – Philippines
  - ✓ Shirts – China
- ❑ Haggar
  - ✓ Shirts – Bangladesh
  - ✓ Shorts – Indonesia
- ❑ Adidas
  - ✓ Hoodie – Columbia
- ❑ Jones New York
  - ✓ Blouse – Thailand
- ❑ New Balance
  - ✓ Shoes – China
  - ✓ Shoes – U.S.A.
- ❑ Mossimo Supply Co.
  - ✓ Shoes – China
- ❑ Merona
  - ✓ Shoes – China
- ❑ Champion
  - ✓ Shoes – China
- ❑ Cherokee
  - ✓ Shoes – China
  - ✓ Shorts – Bangladesh
  - ✓ Polos – Indonesia
- ❑ Circo
  - ✓ T-shirts – Guatemala

Electronics

- ❑ Belkin Router – China
- ❑ Epson Printer Ink – Indonesia
- ❑ HP Printer Ink – Malaysia
- ❑ Panasonic Phone Set – China
- ❑ General Electric Stereo Headset – China
- ❑ Texas Instruments Calculator – China
- ❑ Uniden 2-way Radios – Vietnam
- ❑ Belkin Power Strips - China
- ❑ Philips Portable DVD Player – China

Other

- ❑ Swiss Gear Luggage – China
- ❑ Skyline Luggage – China
- ❑ Pyrex Cookware – U.S.A.
- ❑ Proctor & Gamble Calphalon Cookware – China
- ❑ Sunbeam Crock Pot – China
- ❑ Hamilton Beach Food Processor – China
- ❑ Black & Decker Blender – Mexico

15...The Impact of Foreign Outsourcing

Driving Factors

In the past twenty years or so we have seen a significant amount of outsourcing of jobs to foreign countries. It has now gotten to the point where a large percentage of products are manufactured outside the United States for companies that are organized and operating within the our country. For example, retail operations such as Bed Bath and Beyond or Home Depot routinely carry products that are designed within the United States and manufactured in countries like China. The result is a preponderance of made in China items being stocked in these stores in the U.S.

The driving force behind such outsourcing is usually the cost of labor in this country versus China. While the problem is not unique to China, I will use them as an example in order to simplify the discussion. It's a fact that most companies in the United States have competition. And one of the factors in competition is the price at which the goods are sold. Furthermore, the companies are usually owned by shareholders who are anxious to see good profitability reported each quarter. As a result of these two factors the companies seek lower cost of labor, and China and other foreign countries represent such an opportunity.

A second factor influencing the decision to manufacture in a country like China concerns the prevalence of available financial resources that will be invested in the tooling necessary for efficient manufacturing, another important aspect of keeping costs down.

The combination of these factors makes it easy for a company to decide to outsource their manufacturing. Profitability improves and quality is usually acceptable (that has not always been the case). The lower cost of labor, of course, is possible because of the lower standard of living of the workers in China. China is clearly a developing country and the manufacturing opportunities that result from foreign outsourcing provide a way for the workers to improve their living conditions. Even so, their standard of living is lower – consider the workers assembling Apple's iPad and iPhone, living in company dormitories.

It is relatively easy to observe this process in action. Visit any of your local stores and look at the fine print as to where the products are made. Then observe that the products are fully labeled with the name of the company in the U.S. So you have a U.S. product meeting the needs of the U.S. market and being manufactured in a low labor cost country such as China. The result of course is a severe loss of jobs in the United States.

This outsourcing process has been an ongoing process for a number of years. The balance of trade numbers show that, for many years, imports have far exceeded exports.

Effect on Inflation

There is a side effect to the problems of outsourcing to foreign countries that is not so readily identified. With goods being manufactured in foreign countries with very low cost labor, the host company is in the position of having improved profits. In a competitive environment they are in the position of being able to sell the goods at a lower price than what otherwise would have been possible. The net result is that inflation has been masked.

If you follow the economic news in our country you'll observe that inflation has been moderate for the last 20 years or so.[34] Target inflation rates as defined by the Federal Reserve are often quoted as being in the vicinity of less than 4% per year. And the country has, for the most part, been able to meet these targets (not always, as in the Carter years). That gives the public a comfortable feeling with respect to the value of any funds that they may have saved. I would submit that the real rate of inflation has been significantly understated because the costs associated with goods that have been manufactured outside of the U.S. have been included in the inflation measurement.

You might argue that the lower costs that have been achieved are real and therefore that the measure of inflation is more or less accurate. The problem with that thought process is that eventually outsourced products will become more expensive as countries like China establish a higher standard of living. The labor rates will then go up. The cost of goods manufactured outside of the United States will rise significantly and we will then see the true nature of inflation that is occurring.

---

[34] The average annual inflation rate over the last 20 years has been approximately 3%. It averaged 10% per year under the Carter administration.

A secondary way of looking at this problem is to examine our cost of living over the last few years wherein you ignore goods manufactured outside of the country and focus on goods and services provided within the country. Examine for example, the rate of increase of legal fees, of medical expenses, of accounting expenses, and housing. These are a truer measure of inflation within the country because residents of our country perform the work.

Effects of Outsourcing

We have looked at the driving factors that cause manufacturers to utilize foreign outsourcing, and recognize two major characteristics of this process. The first is for the companies themselves. With lower costs of manufacturing and/or selling prices (that provide a competitive edge) the companies can show better growth and better profitability, factors which enhance the value of their stock. In a competitive environment and with public shareholders the pressure is on these companies to perform by showing good growth and good profitability.

It is very difficult for these companies to willfully decide to utilize labor within the United States and incur the higher labor costs. In fact, most public companies have a legal responsibility to operate in a way that maximizes shareholder value. This problem is further exemplified by noting that several states have now passed legislation that allows individuals to create benefit corporations. These benefit corporations are allowed to have bylaws that allow the companies to place other objectives in front of profitability.

The second characteristic associated with foreign out-sourcing has to do with the loss of jobs, which is, after all, the primary point of discussion in this book. Companies operating with foreign outsourcing retain their administrative, marketing and sales and service staffs within this country, but the manufacturing staff has been outsourced to foreign countries. I believe this is a significant factor in our country's arriving at such a high underemployment rate at this point in time. The jobs lost are not recoverable unless these companies find the motivation, financial or otherwise, to bring manufacturing back to the United States. Even if such motivation can be put in place in a timely manner, it is highly likely that investment must be undertaken on the part of these companies to modernize tooling and manufacturing facilities; thus, another task in the development of an impoverished society.

Trade Barriers

You might conclude we should have put trade barriers in place long before this to prevent the foreign outsourcing that is taking place. That seems like a logical approach, but has the downside that countries like China would likely put in place their own trade barriers for importation of our goods, thus limiting our ability to export products manufactured in the United States. This has been the predominant argument used by various administrations in setting up free trade agreements between countries. The argument put forth by many public companies has been that we have more to gain by exporting to these countries then we lose by exporting jobs.

This argument has been put forth by the high-tech sector. These folks have argued that our technology is superior in the world market and that the export opportunities will therefore be available to these companies. This argument currently does not hold up very well when we see companies like General Electric moving their manufacturing to the countries that represent the market for their new products.[35] This type of outsourcing certainly runs counter to the concept that free trade agreements will be better for this country in the long run, in that they allow us a greater degree of export.

This process of moving manufacturing jobs overseas has led economists and our political leaders to expound at length on the need for folks in this country to recognize that we are moving toward a service economy. They state that we should therefore gear our educational programs to support this hypothesis. We should just agree with the hypothesis and accept the fact that we will not be manufacturing products in the future, but will instead find some other form of work, such as is found in the service industry.

It strikes me that this attitude that we are in a global economy, and that we should support the idea that other countries with lower labor costs should do the manufacturing is not supportive of a healthy, balanced economy in the United States, nor in these other countries.

As stated in a previous chapter the damage that this foreign outsourcing has caused has to a certain extent been masked by the growth of our economy due to the housing bubble. This generated increases in employment that masked the fact that employment was disappearing as manufacturing moved offshore. In a sense we have been lulled into believing

---

[35] G.E. has long been an internationally based company. For example, its medical imaging division has been headquartered in France for many years.

the proposition that outsourcing is good for companies in this country and therefore good for the nation.

I also pointed out, in Chapter 7, that as of 2012 there is an imbalance in the available (unemployed) workforce, heavily tilted towards those that only have a high school degree. This gives us further motivation to build on jobs for those folks, the types of jobs that have been lost to foreign outsourcing.

Towards a Solution

I believe that it is time for us as a nation to reassess this hypothesis. While correcting the problem is obviously not going to be simple, I really believe that we need to re-examine the assumption that we should no longer manufacture in this country. I realize this statement carries with it the suggestion that one needs to re-examine trade barriers but there are other ways in which the federal government can guide the process toward returning manufacturing back to the United States.

The government has various tools at its disposal that can set trends on foreign outsourcing. Trade barriers are an obvious method but one can also consider tax incentives, job placement incentives, etc.

I do not profess to be an expert on how to solve this problem but I firmly believe that we need to see manufacturing come back to the United States. I'm firmly convinced that this is a significant source of our unemployment problem.

The change I'm suggesting runs counter to the current thought process on what our role should be in a global economy; that it is permissible to see manufacturing occur in one country and services to be provided in another. I'm suggesting that a better economic model for countries of the world is to have balance in their own economies with respect to manufacturing and services. That does not mean that every country in the world must be able to manufacture automobiles for example. Some are clearly too small to be able to afford such ventures, but I am saying that as a general principle a country is better off with a balanced economy, and is probably also better off from the security viewpoint in that it cannot be held hostage by other countries for lack of certain products.

I guess what I'm saying is that the previous model, wherein developing countries could raise their standard of living by providing cheap labor to build products that will be sold in the United States is out of date. I believe a better model for these developing countries is to develop their own economies in much the same way as I am suggesting we should be developing ours. They will need to find the financial resources necessary to develop their economies,[36] but when they complete the task they will have balanced economies and they will have their people working for Living Wages.

Another argument made in favor of foreign outsourcing revolves around the benefit we provide to third world developing countries by providing these employment opportunities. I suggest that a better model for helping these

---

[36] This places a burden on these countries in that they do not necessarily have people ready to invest internally. Investment by other countries has the potential to raise their employment and standards of living.

countries is to encourage private sector investment in their commerce activities. Properly made, these investments will help these countries expand their economies and the standard of living for their people.

The disastrous earthquake that recently struck Haiti provided such an opportunity. The country ended up with a huge shortage of housing. That was, and probably still is, an opportunity for foreign investment in housing for the people of Haiti. The investment can be particularly effective if those managing the construction employ Haitians (at a Living Wage, of course) for the construction work.

I would further back up this hypothesis by looking at developing countries and their efforts to provide low cost labor, so that products can be exported to the United States. In this case look closely at the folks who are the employees. I looked, for example, at ongoing discussions in Nicaragua last year where an increase in the minimum wage was being considered.

In that country the minimum wage at the time was well below the poverty level. Some of the more vocal segments of business in that country were concerned that raising these meager wages by 10% would put the clothing companies, whose main business was export, at a severe competitive disadvantage. So you have a discussion going on regarding employees who were working at very low wages such that they cannot afford to purchase the clothing that they manufacture. That same clothing is exported to the United States and because of its low cost garners significant market share, blocking the manufacture of such clothing in the U.S.

To again state the counterargument the question becomes, "Isn't work at some wage, however low, better than no work at all for individuals living in poverty?" I would maintain that as long as we adopt that attitude, without pushing hard for Living Wages in the long term, we are just trying to make folks living in poverty a little more comfortable. Harsh words, I know, but I see this logic applied over and over in impoverished societies, and when such policies trap people in poverty, we've got the wrong approach.

As an aside, since I'm challenging the wisdom of assuming that low wages are better than no wages, why not go a little further. Another characteristic of impoverished societies is that they attract sympathy from the "haves." You see this all the time in actions taken to help the poor in the U.S., and in impoverished countries around the world. Many of these actions are really significant in saving lives (clean water initiatives, for example) and in improving lives (low cost cell phones, for example).

In other words, "We can do a lot of good by designing and manufacturing goods that can be afforded by those living in poverty." I submit that these actions and programs are important and valuable, but that programs that develop their societies should accompany them. Such development programs should be designed to lift people out of poverty so that there is much less need for the assistance programs.

As you might sense, I'm for holding out for solutions that solve the unemployment problems wherever they occur, and that result in nearly all folks earning Living Wages.

Government Incentives

In arguing for manufacturing in the United States, as opposed to foreign outsourcing, I'm not suggesting that we pass laws that require U.S. companies to manufacture in the United States. Such an approach makes no sense from the free enterprise viewpoint. I'm also not suggesting that the government put subsidies into place to enable companies in the U.S. to manufacture competitively.

I do suggest, however, that the government is in the position to provide incentives for companies in the United States to manufacture in this country. For example, one might consider an incentive system centered on the corporate income tax rate. The current maximum corporate tax rate in the U.S. is set at 35%. We should consider offering the incentive of setting the corporate tax rate at some lesser number for those companies manufacturing in the U.S.[37] Such an incentive program would give companies the ability to decide on their own whether it is better to manufacture in the United States, or to use foreign outsourcing. This approach remains consistent with free market capitalism, but at the same time, places an incentive on many companies in the U.S. to do their manufacturing in this country.

There is precedent for this type of incentive that has been in place in this country for some time. This is the R&D tax credit. For years, our government has been encouraging research and development by granting tax credits for funds spent on R&D. This re-categorizes the R&D monies spent from an expense (tax deductible) to a tax credit. The net result is improved income for the company. Such a tax credit has been put in place, as an incentive for companies to increase their research and development, with the theory that

---

[37] A differential of 10% might be in order, perhaps more.

increased R&D will result in better growth for the companies, and thus increased employment.

The above incentive is suggested in general terms. Clearly, one needs to develop the idea in more detail, including the magnitude of tax rate savings that might be granted to those companies manufacturing in the U.S. One feature that can be incorporated into the incentive program is to set the corporate tax rates in such a manner that total tax revenue to the government can actually increase when companies do the manufacturing at home. This can come about through the increase in tax revenues from the employees that would otherwise not be working in the U.S. As they say in the U.S. Congress, the program could conceptually be revenue neutral, perhaps even resulting in higher revenue for the government.

An additional approach to encouraging companies to manufacture in the U.S. would be to lower the corporate income tax rate for all companies. The U.S. has one of the highest corporate tax rates in the world, and we are saddled with a very high underemployment rate. This high corporate tax rate puts the country at a disadvantage in the global economy. This is a further government-induced complication that leads to foreign outsourcing. Just lowering the corporate tax rate for all companies should encourage these companies to consider manufacturing in the U.S. as they will be more price competitive.

Made in the U.S.A.

There is, of course, one final method of causing a shift in this foreign outsourcing. That is to encourage the citizens of this country to vote one more time, this time when they are shopping, to establish their own "Made in the USA" policy. I know that the counterargument to this approach is put forth by those who would say that folks are already in a poor financial position, and having them pay more for their goods just exasperates the problem. But I would suggest that if we are moving towards greatly reduced unemployment and we're moving towards seeing Living Wages being paid in this country, then, that economic burden may not be as bad as it seems. Achieving the goal may be worth the cost.

Some folks already make such a buying decision when they can. One example of this concerns the purchase of shoes from New Balance. The New Balance Company advertises how its shoes are made and where they are made. Not all of their products are made completely in the United State, but they strive to use U.S. labor whenever possible. The New Balance Company is proud of the fact that they manufacture many of their products in the United States and they so state in their advertising and in literature provided with their shoes.

An approach like this requires knowledge on the part of the buyer so that they can determine which products are, in fact, made in the United States. This suggests that a Made in the USA campaign might be effective in some sense in changing the buying habits of our citizens.

This does not take new laws, or policies or new regulations. It requires participation on the part of citizens to request that companies advertise which of their products are made in the USA. We might see a surprising result. This might seem like a small effect with the volunteer effort but it may take such an effort to correct our unemployment problems.

By making this suggestion, I am not suggesting that the public boycott companies that foreign outsource their manufacturing. This is completely counter to the American way and would wrongly penalize companies that conceptually have the very best of non-economic reasons as to why they do their manufacturing outside of the U.S. A program that just provides visibility to the average purchaser, enabling them to decide on their own which products they will purchase, is a much fairer way of encouraging manufacturing in the U.S. without demanding such. Most products sold in the U.S. now carry country of origin statements. I'm suggesting increased visibility.

One of the attractive features of providing information that allows individuals to buy products that are Made in the U.S.A. is that such buying preferences get expressed as market demand, allowing companies to decide on their own how to meet such market demand.[38] It keeps the government out of the business of trying to control how companies manufacture, but lets companies decide on their own their best path to profitability. The country benefits tremendously from free market capitalism when companies respond to the needs in the marketplace without control by the government. This is woven into the basic fabric of our economy and needs to be preserved in the process of working to reduce the high rate of unemployment in this country.

While I'm suggesting the Made in the USA approach as a possible way to encourage manufacturing of goods in the

---

[38] As of this writing, there are many U.S. companies that manufacture in the U.S. and achieve a healthy business in domestic and foreign sales.

U.S., it's not at all clear how effective such a program would be. In particular at this time our economy is not in the best shape and individuals making purchasing decisions are likely to be heavily influenced by lowest possible cost, as opposed to supporting the idea that the product is Made in the U.S.A. An incentive program, of course, as outlined previously is most likely the better solution and it is one that, if properly implemented, may in fact provide lower prices in the long run, which would then enable folks to make their Made in the USA decision on an economic basis.

16...What About Imports?

For purposes of discussion, I'm differentiating between foreign outsourcing and imports. I've previously discussed foreign outsourcing and the effects that it has on our economy by basically having products that would normally be manufactured within the U.S. be manufactured in foreign countries. Imports are products that are developed and manufactured in a foreign country and are imported by import organizations for sale in the US.

Agricultural

As the global economy has developed, importation of agricultural products into the United States is a growing business. Such imports provide an availability of agricultural products that may not be available in the United States due to the timing of the growing season. As such these products do not undermine the employment situation in the U.S.

On the other hand we also have importation of agricultural products that are grown during the same or similar seasons. These imports have typically been harvested with low cost labor, and even with the cost of transportation, represent market-undercutting products. In a sense they have the same effect on the economy, as does foreign outsourcing, namely reducing employment opportunities in the U.S.[39] These imports carry with them an equally important secondary threat.

The importation of agricultural products harvested and packed by low cost labor can have the effect of decimating an entire agricultural segment in the United States. The importation of apples, for example, makes it nearly impossible for apple farmers in the Northwest to earn a profitable living. The threat here, besides the loss of employment, is that the capability for providing those agricultural products, namely apples, will gradually disappear. If, in the future the low cost labor foreign providers see significance increases in their own labor costs, they will be in the position to dictate prices for the products in the market as it has been deprived of competition. Furthermore, if relations with supplying countries deteriorate to the point that the foreign suppliers are prohibited from shipping product to the U.S, we will find ourselves in the position of having a severe shortage of the products.

Agricultural products move both ways in the global economy. In this case we are dealing with nutrition for all, and need to be careful as to the consequences of trying to protect U.S. agriculture from foreign imports. It is reasonable to expect that the government should protect against dumping, but the free trade aspects of agricultural products are important to everyone. Agricultural products, by their

---

[39] With the advent of free trade agreements with countries like Columbia, the imports put pressure on U.S. growers to be more efficient in growing and getting their products to market. Small farmers join cooperatives that lower cost of distribution in order to compete more effectively.

nature, are subject to drought, for example. The global import/export activity largely mitigates the effect of such occurrences.

This problem of importation of agricultural products is further complicated by the fact that farm labor in the United States is provided, to a great extent, by foreign workers residing in this country. To the farmer these folks represent a source of low-cost labor, which they view to be important, if not essential to maintaining their profitability.

The idea that we should move toward paying farm workers a Living Wage further complicates the problem. Implementation of a Living Wage program would clearly raise costs to the farmers that, in turn, would be passed on to the consumer.

In many commodities the solution to problems of high cost labor, and competition from others has led to the implementation of farm subsidies. This, in principle, may ease the problem with respect to the farmer but it places a burden on the taxpayers to effectively support the profitability of farmers.

Other Foreign Products

The United States imports many other products from foreign countries. When these products are unique to these countries we represent an expanded market for these countries. These unique products include cultural items, tourist items, certain brands of beverages, etc. In general it would seem that we should not be as concerned about these imports as we are with those that undercut products that are or could be manufactured in the United States. These products, in fact are a healthy part of the global economy, and provide the opportunity for developing countries to improve their economic condition.

Free trade agreements between the U.S. and other countries offer the chance for true global competition. History has shown that it is a healthy competition; witness the effect Japan has had on auto quality. Once Japan realized the importance of the quality of their exports, they began to challenge the U.S. auto industry with higher quality products. This, in turn, has forced the U.S. manufacturers to turn to improving quality – the U.S. consumer benefits.

17...Inflation or Price Corrections?

On Inflation

In the foregoing, we have suggested a number of actions that need to be taken if we are to have any success at all in attacking the problem of unemployment in this country. Many of the suggested actions have the potential to increase the labor content of the cost of goods for products manufactured in this country. A logical question to ask is, "What effect will this have on the price of goods available to the public, and will in fact such actions result in rather severe inflation?"

Certainly a gradual move toward implementation of Living Wages for full-time employees will result in higher labor costs for those products. The argument can be made that these higher prices place a burden on the very people were trying to help. I suggest that the benefit of moving to Living Wages far outweighs any price increases on goods and services purchased by those that we are trying to help.

Bringing manufacturing labor back to the United States, in the process of reducing foreign outsourcing, can have a similar effect on the prices of goods sold in this country. In cases where the products are being manufactured in foreign countries with sub-fair wages, it would seem reasonable to live with the price increases in the interest of seeing people rewarded fairly for their work efforts.

On the other hand, if an incentive program is implemented, such as was suggested in the previous chapter, price increases of the products thus manufactured do not necessarily occur. Leverage on prices comes from the government's ability to set corporate tax rates.

A review of inflationary trends within the United States over the past 50 years might prove beneficial to understanding the inflationary effects of these proposed actions. For many years we have been told by our economists and elected officials that inflation, for the most part, has been under control. By under control, we usually envision an inflation rate of 4% per year or less. Based on that inflation criteria, history will tell us that we have avoided any serious inflationary effects during most of this period (except for the Carter years).

Real Inflation

I suggest that the statement that inflation has been under control in this country over this 50-year period is not correct. Inflation is usually measured over a selection of goods and services consumed in the United States. Most of these goods have to do with items that are generally purchased by the public.

During this same period of time we have turned more and more to imports and to foreign outsourcing. This trend has been gradual and extended over a period of time and has had the effect of lowering the prices on many of the items that are included in the inflationary index measurement. The impact of low cost labor in these imports and foreign outsourcing activities has mitigated what otherwise would have been significant increases in prices. Thus the measurement of inflation over this period of time is deceptively low because of the inclusion of these low labor products. Some would say that this is a good thing, that we have "controlled" inflation by turning to foreign, low cost labor. But at what price? Now we have high underemployment in this country. It seems like this method of controlling inflation is not a good thing.

You can better see the nature of the true inflation that has occurred when you examine goods and services that must be manufactured and or performed in the United States. Examples of this include services such as legal fees, accounting fees, and other labor-intensive services that are provided to the public. Another example is the cost of construction of homes in the United States. These types of activities are usually not as subject to the influence of imports and foreign outsourcing (with the exception of some building materials).

Most people are aware of the nearly continual complaints by elected officials that health care costs in the United States are increasing at a much faster rate than the normal rate of inflation. Here again, healthcare must be delivered by folks living in the United States, and is thus giving us a truer measure of inflation. We must, however, be careful to include in the analysis the greatly increased diagnostic and therapeutic capabilities that have been developed over the years that, in fact, raise the price of delivering healthcare at a significant benefit to the patient.

Examination of such inflationary data shows that the rate of inflation has been significantly higher than that published by economists and the federal government and that the increasing healthcare costs are in fact influenced significantly by the inherent real inflation that has been taking place in our economy.

Given the nature of true inflation that has occurred, the recommended actions described above may in fact just reveal to us what the true inflation rate has been. That is, we might have seen significantly higher inflation rates over the past years if we had not turned to imports and foreign out-sourcing techniques to keep prices low.

Price Increases

These are just, perhaps, rationalizations on why we might be willing to accept upward adjustments in the cost of goods manufactured in United States when we implement such measures as Living Wages and when we gradually bring back manufacturing that has been outsourced. Be that as it may, the real issue is, do we want to reduce or eliminate under-employment? That is really the core issue here and I believe that we as a country should be willing to accept price adjustments in the process of reducing underemployment.

Unintended Consequences

In the process of suggesting any change in the policies and regulations that influence our economy, we always need to look for the inevitable unanticipated consequences. Thus far in the discussion of the means by which we may eliminate underemployment, we have focused on a large number of potential actions, including paying Living Wages to full-time employees and bringing manufacturing back to the U.S. Both of these actions have the potential to increase the prices of consumer goods in the United States.[40] An obvious question to ask is, "What effect will these price increases have on the impoverished? After all, it is the impoverished that we're trying to help, and if these programs do nothing but raise the cost of living for these individuals we have failed in our mission."

I have heard repeated discussions with respect to this problem when discussing the salaries of fast food employees. There is an assumption that these individuals rely heavily on fast food restaurants for their nutrition and that raising prices at these restaurants will, in fact, do harm to the individuals. I suggest first of all that one set of employees that will not be negatively affected by possible price increases is the employees of the fast food restaurants themselves. They will have moved from sub-par wages to Living Wages under the program. For these folks, an increase in the cost of fast food meals is a minor inconvenience as compared to the benefit of working for Living Wages.

For others that are classified as living in poverty it is reasonable to examine how serious a problem this might be. While a careful analysis should clearly be conducted, a quick look at the situation shows that it may not a severe problem. If we assume the fast food workers currently earn $10 per hour and the Living Wage is closer to $15 per hour, we would see a 50% increase in the cost of labor that goes into the preparation and serving of fast food. If the labor content of a fast food meal, as calculated based on those employed at

---

[40] Price increases do not always occur when manufacturing is returned to the U.S. Often, investment in more modern tooling results in increased productivity that can preclude the need for price increases.

the fast food restaurant, were 20% of the selling price, then we would see the labor content move upward by five dollars per hour. The result is a 10% increase in the cost of fast food meals if the restaurant is to maintain the same profitability.

The above analysis shows that, as we would expect, increasing wages and maintaining restaurant profitability will result in higher prices for meals over the general population. We need to evaluate the seriousness of this price increase versus the benefit that will accrue to the employees that move from wages that keep them in poverty to Living Wages that provide a much higher quality of life. See the Chapter 11 discussion on Living Wages and income re-distribution for more on this topic.

In the end analysis this discussion shows that programs designed to reduce or eliminate underemployment should really include measures that will lift people out of poverty. In a sense this is the central argument that I am making. I'm suggesting that a key to solving the unemployment problem includes a serious effort to solve the poverty problem. Lifting people out of poverty puts them into the general marketplace, thus increasing demand for goods and services throughout the country.

18...When Perks Get Out of Hand

The Problem

A discussion of government "when perks get out of hand" may seem out of place in a book describing ways in which the United States can recover from this prolonged period of high unemployment, but when we are seeking to increase employment, every job counts.

By way of background, we are at the point with many of our local governments wherein the perks granted by elective boards are seriously impeding the ability of these boards to hire needed workers. Many local government agencies have set up what many would call extravagant retirement and retirement health care programs within their usually severely limited budgets. This has restricted the capability of these boards to hire needed workers.

The problem extends to state and federal governments as well. Elected officials have basically set up very attractive retirement benefit programs for themselves and for their employees. These programs are not available to the average American and therefore are a part of a non-level playing field when it comes to retirement programs approved by the various agencies of the government.

The problem stems in part from the relationship between elected officials and the government employee unions.

Unions have done a lot of good for the workers in this country negotiating with profit-oriented companies. In a negotiation between elected officials and the unions, the profitability factor is missing and the elected officials have not had the incentive to resist extravagant propositions. The net result has been financial difficulty for many of our government agencies, overburdened with retirement and retirement health care costs.[41] The state of California is a prime example of this situation. It is now finding that immense retirement reserves are under-funded.

On a broader basis we find the state and federal governments approving retirement benefit plans for themselves and their employees that are well above plans that are approved by them for the general public. Examples include health care benefits for the working, healthcare benefits paid to the retired, and generous retirement programs. These programs, of course, are one of the costs of operating the government, requiring more tax revenue from the general public, and therefore consuming funds that might otherwise be used to develop our economy to relieve unemployment.

Many of these generous programs were historically set in the place on the theory that government service was not an attractive career. The many perks were granted, including generous vacation time each year, as a basis for hiring "good people" into government positions. The approval by these

---

[41] The problem is not just one of lacking fiscal responsibility. Boards composed of ordinary citizens govern many local agencies. They often struggle with the difficulty of negotiating reasonable contracts and are prone to agreeing to high demands, figuring the next set of elected officials can sort out any problems created.

people of the generous benefit plans has now turned the tables to where the government jobs in many cases are superior in financial reward to jobs in the public marketplace.

As previously noted unions have been of great benefit to many workers in the United States. They function well when there is arms length negotiation between the employer and the unions. When this negotiation is not balanced, union demands can succeed beyond reasonable bounds and financial problems can ensue. A case in point to consider is the coal miner's situation under union leader John L Lewis. In that case the union demands were successful to the point that the coalmines became noncompetitive and were closed down.

More recently we have seen the problem of excessive wages and benefits granted the unions by the automobile manufacturers in the United States. This has been, in part, a cause for the filing of bankruptcy by General Motors and Chrysler. To further validate the point, when the car manufacturers emerged from bankruptcy, they had in place renegotiated contracts with the unions, which resulted in more reasonable wages and benefits, at least for new hires. While this re-write should allow the manufacturers to be competitive in the global marketplace, the jury is still out since many of the benefits for experienced autoworkers were apparently left in place.

The free market environment of the for-profit companies leads eventually to resolution, either through closedown or the filing of bankruptcy. Other companies will then arise to take their place. In the case of the federal government and the state governments we don't have the free market forces at work and excessive perks will remain with these organizations short of filing for bankruptcy. We have two examples of this in California with the bankruptcies filed by Vallejo, and more recently Stockton. These cities are working their way out of bankruptcy with the courts' approval of restructuring of the generous benefit plans that were granted to the employees.

Corrective Trends

In other states political leaders are structuring laws through legislation or the initiative process that will reduce the onerous financial burden placed by these generous perks.

If we are to follow the spirit of the idea of paying employees Living Wages, in part so that they may live a productive life, then we should also look at the pay and benefits that have been self-granted to government employees that are out of line as compared to those available to the general public.

For example, let's look at government employee pensions. With sufficient time served at a given pay grade these pensions are typically granted at 80% to 85% of the latest salary of the individual. From the fiscal accounting viewpoint the government entity needs to set up a retirement fund to be able to fund the pensions.

As we have seen in the recent downturn following the housing bubble, these plans have been structured such that if the invested retirement funds lose value due to a decline in the stock market, for example, the public entity must commit additional funds to the retirement funds. That failsafe pension fund protection is just not available to the average citizen. If the citizen invests money for retirement in the stock market and the stock market declines he/she lives with the loss. Under these generous plans the government employees that incur the same loss in the marketplace expect the government to make up that loss. That is hardly a level playing field between government employees and the general public, and it should be corrected.

Elimination of these extravagant pay scales and perks for government employees will go a long ways toward restoring public confidence in its government and elected officials. It is hard to envision why elected officials and government employees should enjoy such an advantage over the average person. It would seem more reasonable that, if an elected official is going to vote for and approve a health care plan for themselves, for example, then that the same plan with the similar costs to the individual should be available to the average voter.

The same argument applies to pensions. If the average person is encouraged and allowed to set up retirement savings accounts such as IRAs with certain rules as to contributions he or she may make, and what contributions the company may make, then the same pension system should apply to public employees.

19...Environmental Protection

═══

On the Environment

In recent years our citizens and the government have become seriously concerned about environmental protection. Past problems with air quality, water quality and general living conditions have prompted local, state and federal governments to take action to protect the environment. In addition, scientific studies concerning man-made global warming are debated extensively in our country. We will cover the latter in a subsequent chapter.

There's no doubt that there have been environmental problems in the past and that they should be addressed. Water pollution in rivers for example has often occurred. Likewise, air pollution can be a problem in certain areas of the country, depending upon the topography and the weather conditions. The problem that we're having is how to strike a reasonable balance between environmental protection and normal development such as construction of subdivisions dams, roads and pipelines.

The Environmental Protection Agency is continuously upgrading its standards, making it more and more difficult for development to take place. It's easy to understand the motivation behind these laws and regulations. The question is, "How fast do we push regulations that in the end disrupt our economy?" At a time when we have a severe under-employment problem, it would seem inappropriate to be trying to tighten environmental regulations to the extreme. It goes back to the argument of which goal is more important, this time environmental protection versus development. If one allows development one creates jobs and these jobs increase tax revenues. Those tax revenues in turn allow the government more flexibility in trying to achieve its environmental protection goals. It would seem more reasonable to rein in the environmental protection growth until such time as the economy is on a better footing and the unemployment problem is solved.

An obvious example of the exercise of strict environmental protection rules occurred after the BP oil spill in the Gulf of Mexico. Once investigations and the cleanup were completed and it was time to start issuing new drilling permits, the environmental protection regulations were tightened to an extreme, first as a moratorium on new applications, then slowing down development of the oil fields in the Gulf of Mexico. This of course results in reduced employment in that field.

A more recent example of catering to the power of the environmental protection lobby is the Keystone pipeline project. The final link in this pipeline from Canada to the United States is still on hold pending more environmental review. The net result of the delay in approval of the final link of that project is again, reduced employment. This delay also has the detrimental effect, of course, of slowing down our attempts to achieve oil independence from the rest of the world. You might ask why this statement would be appropriate for discussion of underemployment in the United States, but again the economic consequences of the delaying action are significant.[42] The longer this country remains dependent on foreign oil for its energy needs the more vulnerable we are to very high prices and the oil purchases being made at these high prices drain funds from the United States.

The most current example of the increasing influence of environmental protection is concerned with coal-fired power plants. As of the writing of this book, the EPA has issued draft regulations on air quality surrounding coal-fired power plants that will, according to industry sources, cause a number of these power plants to be shut down. Once again, the priority seems to be placed on environmental protection with no regard to the economics of the situation and the underemployment problem.

In the environmental protection area we also have to deal with the endangered species act. We see more and more endangered species being added to the list. This is all well and good, but it can have a detrimental effect on employment. In California, the most recent example of this is concerned with the shipment of water from the Northern California Delta region to the Central Valley (for farming) and to Southern California for support of the population.

Water flows through the viaduct systems have been severely restricted by court order in trying to protect the

---

[42] The argument is not that we should ignore environmental protection. The problem centers on the extreme delays that are introduced by extensive environmental review. We have an employment problem in the U.S., and need to be efficient wherever we can in resolving problems so that development can move forward.

Delta smelt (*hypomesus transpacificus*). Operators of the water system have attempted to install screens that will prevent any damage to the Delta smelt but these efforts have not been successful. The net result is that the Delta smelt is being protected over farm activity in the central valley of California and over the needs of the population in Southern California.

In this project the pumping system and aqueduct system pull water from the Northern California Delta region for use by farmers in the Central Valley and the people of Los Angeles. These systems were installed after review and approval by the government, and resulted in the establishment of more farms in the Central Valley and the support of more people in the Los Angeles region. To now say, oops, we did not mean to give you that approval seems to be an incorrect way to propagate environmental protections. Because these farms are established and the people do live in Los Angeles, we now come to the point, as acknowledged by at least one federal judge that we need to figure out who is the endangered species; the farmers and the people of Los Angeles or the smelt?

What Can We Do?

I believe that environment protection is one of the more difficult areas to reconcile with the need to develop our economy to solve the unemployment problem. Taken individually a lot of the environmental regulations appear to have reasonable merit and it is not easy to decide that such regulation should be delayed or canceled. On the other hand we've got a lot of unemployed people, looking for work, and expecting that investment will be made by private enterprise in order to achieve growth.

I would suggest that at this time, because we have so many of our people living in poverty with underemployment rates in the vicinity of 15%, that we need to delay implementation of all of the newly discovered environmental protection ideas. The slow-down of this type can occur by beginning at the top with the federal government's regulations. States and local agencies can contribute to the process of controlling the environmental regulations to a reasonable level by establishing laws that strike a balance between the need for development and the need for environmental protection.

A lot of people would say that industry and private investors have had plenty of time to bring environmental protection into the equation when pursuing development projects. If we delay implementation of some of the environmental protection ideas, then we are again putting off what should have been accomplished by now. It would appear to me that the country is in somewhat of a crisis mode at this time because of the unemployment problem and is not a good idea to let this problem linger for many years.

Some say that we can have our environmental protection regulations and still have some development. It won't be that detrimental to the development world, and it will bring environmental protections in that we would like to see. One could go so far as to say, "All right, duly noted. We should have been developing with better environmental protection long before this." But that ignores the real unemployment problem that we have and to think that this is the time when we should tighten up all of the environmental protection regulations ahead of economic development does not seem wise.

This is probably an area where there is a trade-off between the timing with which environmental regulations are established and the approval of development projects that will provide significant additional employment. I would suggest that we are beginning to realize the severe harm that high underemployment causes. From the economics view-point continued high unemployment results in continued high expenditures by the government with its programs of unemployment support. These continued expenses occur in parallel with a reduced level of tax revenue to the government because of the high number of unemployed. This results in a larger and larger deficit for the country and the resulting negative economic consequences.

Unemployment is also a critical problem with our young people in the 18 to 25-year-old age bracket. These folks are just coming into the labor market at a terrible time with very limited opportunity. This puts these people in the position of trying to decide how they can move forward in life and presents to them the temptations associated with the underground economy and illegal activities such as the selling of drugs.

I therefore come to the bottom line conclusion that at the present time environmental protection policies and regulations should be eased, or at least the growth of those policies and regulations should be eased in favor of allowing development that will result in employment opportunities. I do not believe that this will cause irreparable damage to the environment and also believe that once the economy has recovered, there will be the opportunity for orderly establishment of further environmental protections. With our high deficit spending, we are much better off in recovering our economy first. That approach then gives us better funding for government activities, without the need for further indebtedness.

20...Man-Made Global Warming

A Debatable Topic

Man-made global warming is the subject of extensive debate, worldwide. There are those who believe that man-made global warming is occurring and that everyone should be seriously concerned about the effects of global warming, to the point that policies and regulations should be put into place immediately to attempt to mitigate the effects thereof.

Man-made global warming is a difficult subject to analyze, given the difficulty in predicting what will happen in the future that would not otherwise happen. In the popular press man-made global warming is blamed for increased hurricane activity or decreased hurricane activity. It is currently blamed for the hot spell spreading crossed the Midwest in the United States. The subject is much too complex to include a rigorous analysis in favor of or against the argument in this book.

Setting Priorities

It is appropriate however, to discuss the effects of existing and proposed global warming policies and regulations on economic development of an impoverished society. In cases of extreme poverty, such as that encountered in countries like Nicaragua, it is obvious to me that one needs to strike a balance between actions intended to prevent man-made global warming and the welfare of persons living in poverty. Trying to correct conceived problems that have occurred over many, many years by penalizing individuals that are just trying to lift themselves out of poverty, makes absolutely no sense.

How to extrapolate that position to development of the economy in the United States is not readily obvious. Because of the advanced state of our style of living in this country, we can more readily accommodate some programs that are designed to limit emissions that, we believe, are the cause of man-made global warming.

However, we still have the need to balance our efforts to prevent man-made global warming with the real need to develop an impoverished society. This suggests that local governments, federal government, and state governments need to be practical in setting policies and standards.[43] This is particularly true when the policy and standards become a financial burden on potential developments that are designed to lift people out of poverty. Local governments bear a significant responsibility in setting these policies and standards.

---

[43] Those that promote the concept that global warming is occurring, and that it is at least in part man-made, have significant influence in government. Witness California's cap and trade policy, put in place by the state government at a time when the state is in very bad financial condition, with a severely unbalanced budget. (A policy promoted at the Federal level, but not approved by Congress.)

21...What About Developing Countries?

Side Effects of our Policies

In the foregoing, we made the case that in many instances we, as a country need to get back our manufacturing capability, and we made the case without much discussion as to the potential side effects such a policy would have on developing countries. There will very likely be side effects of such a policy that will affect the economies of developing countries, in particular where these countries are exporting products to the United States based on the use of very low cost labor. In other circumstances, where employees receive a reasonable wage for their efforts in these countries, one could see the emergence of healthy competition on a global basis.

Certainly new products that are developed in the United States and are manufactured in this country will have minimal impact on other countries since manufacturing will not be moving from those countries back to the United States. This, in fact, is probably the most efficient means of reestablishing manufacturing in the United States, because it does not involve retooling for products previously manufactured outside our borders.

On the other hand, in cases where manufacturing has

already been outsourced to foreign countries, there will be more impact on the countries doing the manufacturing. This can have a serious impact on those countries that are manufacturing goods for companies in the United States, based on their low labor costs or favorable currency valuations.

In a theoretical sense countries that might be affected in such a negative way could work their way out of the negative impact by implementing wage policies within their country, similar to the model suggested herein. That is to say if these countries can garner development funds that will allow them to develop their own economies and in the process pay Living Wages, markets within their countries can be satisfied by companies that are manufacturing within their own country. I use the word theoretical because in practice, it may be difficult for developing countries to secure funding that will allow them to develop their own economies and sell in their own markets.

In the end it boils down to our country making the decision as to whether we should be subsidizing other countries in the world that are manufacturing with the payment of sub-fair wages. In particular, do we wish to continue our own relatively high rate of unemployment in the interest of helping companies in these countries achieve profits utilizing sub fair wage employees?

The argument has been put forth by many that, in fact, it is un-American for us to insist on Made in America policies. Those that argue this point contend that in a global economy it really doesn't matter where the manufacturing is taking place. They acknowledge that it does involve the loss of manufacturing jobs in the United States, but that these jobs should just be replaced by other jobs such as those in a service economy.

The argument would be easier to accept if we did not have a track record of what has happened when we do foreign outsourcing. If we accept the fact that the housing bubble and associated ramping up of the economy in fact masked the effects of foreign outsourcing, then it's hard to agree with this idea that it really doesn't matter where the manufacturing is done.

I do not propose that our government should require companies to manufacture in the United States. This tramples on the idea of free market capitalism and can lead to the government making decisions as to what products are made, where they are made and at what price they should be sold. It's extremely important that we preserve our free market capitalism, and that any transfer of manufacturing back to the United States be done on the basis of incentives that offer better economic opportunity for at least some companies, but at the same time preserve their freedom of choice.

Some Examples

In recent years we have seen much of our clothing manufacturing transferred to developing countries. Our government has set import policies that make it attractive for companies to basically outsource the manufacturing to these developing countries.

I'll go back to the situation in Nicaragua to illustrate how this is working. Nicaragua has a significant clothing manufacturing operation that exports its products worldwide and in particular to the United States. They also have a

Minimum Wage Council composed of union, government and private enterprise representatives. In late 2011, there were ongoing discussions about raising the minimum wage from approximately $.75 per hour to approximately $.90 per hour. There was serious concern on the part of the clothing manufacturing companies that such an increase in the cost of labor would put them at a serious competitive disadvantage in the world marketplace. In that country, wages below one dollar an hour clearly place the employee below the poverty line. So, the manufacturers are suggesting that in order for them to compete in the world marketplace, their employees should be kept (in a sense) in poverty. This problem is likely not unique to Nicaragua.

Once again, we are faced with the issue; is this what we want to see in the global economy? The argument, of course, is that some wage is better than no wage for these employees. A better approach, it seems to me, would be for these countries to focus on how they can develop their economies so that the employees in these countries can at least have wages that place them above the poverty line. Such development, of course, will require financial resources that may or may not be available in country.

A South American country illustrated another example of how developing countries might solve their economic problems. I believe it was Columbia that decided to not allow the importation of smart cell phones, unless some degree of manufacturing of these devices was carried out in Columbia. Here's an example of a country, realizing that they need to have their citizens employed, working out a practical solution on how to add value to the manufacturing of the cell phones. The net result was a delay in the availability of the cell phones in the country, but realization of the benefit of employment for a significant number of citizens.[44]

Finally, we have the example of Apple manufacturing its iPhone and other products in China. Apple's profits from the sale of the products have been impressive and have no doubt been enhanced by the use of low-cost labor in China. The number of people employed in the manufacture of the iPhone alone is amazing.

Recently, activists have questioned Apple's use of low-cost labor on the assumption that those building the Apple products in China are somehow abused. Apple has undertaken continuous review of the contract manufacturers' procedures and policies with respect to their employees and has concluded that, while there might have been some problems, the current environment for these employees is acceptable.   The employees of at least one of the manufacturers live in dormitories at the factories.   This clearly does not result in Living Wages for these employees. So, we in this country gain the benefit of relatively low cost Apple products off the backs of the Chinese employees. Welcome to the global economy.

There are steps these countries can take, such as that taken by Columbia, to develop their economies to improve their standard of living. Development of their economies is key. Attracting foreign investment allows establishment of enterprises that employ people. Payment of fair wages can

---

[44] A policy of maximizing in-country value added when products must be imported has a very positive influence on building up employment in the country.

result in products that can be exported and can successfully be part of the global economy (without dumping).

Maximizing value added for products that must be imported helps improve the local employment, such as was the case in Columbia with cell phones.

22...To Summarize the Problem

The History

Let's now stand back and look at what has happened in the last 40 years or so.

- ❑ Emerging, developing countries discover that they can manufacture goods and sell them in the U.S.

- ❑ American companies find that they can improve their profits by out sourcing manufacturing to foreign countries with low cost labor. Manufacturing starts to leave the country.

- ❑ Meanwhile, Congress decides that only the rich own homes. That's not fair, so they push to solve the problem by lowering loan qualification standards for lower income folks. Say hello to the sub-prime mortgage.

- ❑ Thus begins the housing boom. The attendant construction activity masks the departure of manufacturing jobs to foreign countries. All is well in hood!

- ❑ The flurry of activity in the housing construction segment fuels the emergence of the green movement. The sky's the limit on housing costs so we add home sprinkler system requirements, low water use toilets, solar on the roof, purple water for the garden and mini-sewer plants in place of septic tank systems, to name a few.

- ❑ Next, the banks wake up - the sub-primes are worthless. So, they bundle them with prime mortgages and re-sell the packages. As foreclosures begin, the true value of the packages becomes apparent and "the walls came tumbling down."
- ❑ So, we have the politicians pushing for fairness in home ownership by lowering loan qualification standards and the environmentalists demanding high cost initiatives to "save the earth."

What Did We Get?

- ❑ A global financial crisis.
- ❑ 15 % underemployment in the U.S.
- ❑ Government spending and deficits going out of sight to shore up the 46 million folks living in poverty.
- ❑ 23 million or so folks out of work, another 8 million working part time.
- ❑ Record numbers of people on food stamps.
- ❑ Record numbers of people on social security disability.

What Did We Achieve?

- ❑ LESS home ownership for low-income families.
- ❑ Worse restrictions on loan qualification requirements, further restricting low-income home ownership.
- ❑ Tighter banking rules that inhibit economic recovery.
- ❑ Continued push to "save the earth" regardless of the cost.

Free market capitalism in the U.S. worked for 200+ years. Then all these initiatives and tighter regulations have come in to stymie recovery from the recession. Ah ha, we say, free market capitalism (the old way) no longer works. Let's try something new.

No, why not revert to that which did work? We don't need something new, we need to re-adjust and/or eliminate the factors that are blocking recovery. We know the underlying principles that do work, based on our history.

It's time to intelligently accelerate economic recovery.

23...To Achieve Economic Recovery

The Task of Creating Jobs

There is an urgent need to solve the unemployment problems that currently exist in the United States. The country is faced with high deficit spending, in part because of the reduced workforce. By solving the job creation problem, one also makes progress in solving the deficit problem by providing more tax revenue to the government. In the following sections, we discuss steps that can be taken that should result in a significant number of new jobs and lead us to economic recovery.

Our goal should be to return at least to levels of employment that existed prior to the financial meltdown that occurred after the housing bubble burst. The ultimate measure, however, should be the unemployment rate. And, I would suggest that to gauge success that the underemployment rate should be at an acceptably low level in most if not all segments of our society. We cannot consider our job creation program a success if we are left with pockets of high underemployment, such as that which currently exists among young urban black people, for example.

Note that the list is long. Some actions will have high payout, others more moderate. But in our current position, we need to look at all of them as we strive to get people back to work by developing our economy. Economic development requires investment, and many of the actions suggested herein are made in the interest of providing a vibrant investment environment so that free market capitalism can bring us out of this economic malaise.[45]

The suggestions made here have been made by many, and politicians have varying views as to the probability of their success. This is your chance to elect officials that understand the origins of our economic problems and that understand the history of capitalism and how our country came to be the success it is in the world.

A Free Market Capitalist Society.

Free market capitalism historically has propelled the United States into its prominent position amongst world economies. This model has worked well from the standpoint of advancing our standard of living and producing more and more innovative products that are sold worldwide.

Therefore, when evaluating methods of increasing employment in our country, we should keep in mind that which has been successful in the past and build upon that experience. The free market model has the advantage that individuals strive to improve their lives and in the process they create economic activity in the country that improves life for all.

---

[45] With ongoing national discourse on "fairness" one might conclude that this proposal just makes the wealthy richer. My point; the wealthy have the funds that must be invested to grow the economy. The folks are the ones that achieve a better life (with good employment) when the wealthy take the risk of investing in our economy.

The government has a role to play in our society, primarily as a guide on the free enterprise process. We don't expect the government to be the creator of all new jobs nor to replace free market capitalism in the country. In fact, limitations on the growth of government and the intrusion of the government into our daily lives are necessary if the free market capitalist model is to function efficiently. We have seen numerous examples of over-regulation in recent years that have, in fact, slowed progress in the growth of our economy.   It is not easy for the government to act with restraint, especially when responding to pressure groups.

How Jobs are Created in our Society

Jobs are created in our economy when there is increased market demand for goods and services and individuals and companies are able to respond to these market needs by increasing production and/or starting new companies. The key words here are, "able to respond." This is another way of saying that the economic environment must be favorable for investment by these individuals and companies. Without such favorable economic conditions, we can find ourselves in difficult situations with high unemployment. The fact is that many factors have to be lined up to create the right environment for investment.

As stated, our system relies on free enterprise investment as a means of establishing new companies and expanding the business of existing companies. Investment will occur by outsiders if the risk reward conditions are favorable. Companies and individuals will make the investments necessary to achieve growth, provided they are not excessively taxed to the point of lacking the funds necessary for investment.

Improving the Educational System

Good education is a critical element in the development of an impoverished society (one with very high under-employment). As a country we need to continue to strive to improve our educational system, which is largely funded at the state level.

The process begins with keeping young people in school at least through the high school level. Without this basic education individuals will indeed have a difficult time finding meaningful employment. Beyond that the system needs to accommodate those that would go on to achieve college degrees and those that would prefer to develop trade skills. The country needs both types of individuals.

In recent years the cost of a college education has increased dramatically, and some question the value of the return on the investment that must be made to receive a college degree. The establishment of community colleges was a step in the right direction toward relieving the cost burden of a college education. It would seem that it would be appropriate to examine other methods by which college degrees can be earned at lesser expense.

Trade schools are an important part of the equation for preparing individuals to enter the workforce. Continued emphasis on ensuring that such facilities are available to young people is important.

When the country is faced with such a large un-employment problem, as currently exists, it would seem reasonable to encourage companies to hire unskilled individuals, and to have them trained on the job. We've previously discussed the importance of paying Living Wage Benefits to employees. One might consider programs where entry-level positions that include training by the companies, would provide a lesser wage during the training period and that the federal government might provide tax credit to the companies for performing the training.

One of the problems in achieving the required education for young people that lack the skills necessary for a particular job is that typically they will have a difficult time in being able to afford further education such as from trade schools or community colleges.[46] Paying the individual during the apprentice period would provide an incentive for the individual to pursue this education and the tax credit provided to the company would provide a financial incentive for them to train these individuals that would otherwise not likely qualify for employment.

Economic Development Incentives

We discussed previously, the need to have an investment friendly economy if we are to undergo development of our economy to solve the unemployment problem. There are a number of initiatives that should be taken that would further enhance the environment for investment.

You might ask the question, "If this is a free market capitalist system, why are you suggesting actions to be taken

---

[46] This problem is going to get more serious the longer the economy stays in this low growth position. The children of the unemployed will grow to enter the workplace with parents unable to provide much if any educational financial support.

by the government or other entities to assist the capitalists?" The answer is that we actually operate with a government constrained free market capitalist system. The government sets up laws, policies and regulations that heavily influence the functioning of our economy.

So, in suggesting that incentives be set up, I'm really just proposing that the laws, policies and regulations be favorable to let the economy grow. This is for the benefit of all, and does not happen automatically. Many incentives are already in use by our governments (local, state and federal) such as the funding of economic development zones and the granting of R&D tax credits to high tech companies. The following incentives are suggested as a means of accelerating the development of our economy.

- ❑ Establish tax incentives for domestic manufacturing. The United States has one of the highest corporate income tax rates among developed countries in the world. At the same time, we have watched our manufacturing be outsourced to foreign countries as a means of maintaining profitability of the manufacturing process.

  It makes no sense for this country to have such a high corporate tax rate when we are competing against countries with lower rates. This suggests that the corporate tax rate should be lowered, and as previously discussed; one should consider a two-tiered corporate tax rate. The higher rate might be set for those whose manufacturing is outsourced and a lower rate might be set for those that manufacture within the United States. Such an incentive would bring back some portion of the manufacturing jobs lost over the past years.

❑ <u>Capital Gains Tax Structure.</u> The 2012 capital gains tax rate was 15%. Congress approved an increase to a maximum 20% for those individuals making over $400,00 income, effective January 1, 2013. This action prevented the rate from increasing to 25% on January 1, 2013 had action not been taken. The Affordable Care Act, however, adds in another 3.8% tax, bringing the total capital gains tax maximum rate to 23.8%. The increases in the capital gains tax rate effective January 1, 2013 will be a significant deterrent to investment that is needed in order to develop the economy to reduce unemployment.

❑ <u>Investment opportunities – rich vs. everyone.</u> In the past the government has worked hard to protect individual investors from the risks of investing in startup companies. This meant that private individuals with low net worth or moderate net worth were not allowed to risk investment in startups. That changed in 2011, with the passage by Congress and approval of the president, Senate Bill number 685, which loosened the restrictions, with regard to individual investment. This is a step in the right direction in that it opens up additional sources of investment capital, which are going to be needed if we are to develop the economy.[47]

---

[47] As of this writing, the administration is delaying implementation of these new rules.

- ❑ <u>SEC Regulations: practical and cost effective – going public to provide reward.</u> As I have discussed, investors that take risk by investing in startup companies need to be able to identify their eventual means of liquidity. It is therefore important that the Securities and Exchange Commission (SEC) operate with rules, policies and procedures that are practical and cost effective. With the high underemployment rate that the country faces, this is not the time to try to achieve the ultimate in shareholder protection by having the SEC lay on onerous layers of rules and regulations.

- ❑ <u>Eliminate or modify Sarbanes-Oxley.</u> The Sarbanes-Oxley act, passed by Congress and signed into law in 1982, was crafted in response to the Enron accounting problems. The Act placed a significant legal and accounting burden on public reporting companies.

  While one could argue about the complications and costs that this act places on public companies, and argue about the effect that it has on our economy, one need only look at various company's responses to this requirement to understand the implications.

  Specifically, we have seen a significant increase in public companies taking themselves private as a means of improving their financial performance, rather than remain under the requirements of Sarbanes-Oxley. This is just one more deterrent that has been put in place by the government, in the interest of trying to achieve the "zero defect society."

Elimination or modification of this law, with an eye towards creating a more investment friendly atmosphere would be a step in the right direction.

❑ Eliminate or revise Dodd-Frank. On July 21, 2010 President Obama signed into law the Dodd-Frank Wall Street Reform and Consumer Protection Act. This law places further restrictions on banks and lending institutions and provides new consumer protection bureaucracy. The law requires new regulations be put into place that will tighten credit restrictions. Generally, the law further restricts banking activity, something we do not need at this time. The law should be revised to eliminate needless restrictions that will tend to put a damper on developing the economy.[48]

❑ Training Incentives. Set up a system of incentives for companies that train the unemployed for new jobs. It is generally recognized that education is the key to reducing unemployment. This is true, of course, provided that there is market demand that justifies increased hiring of these well-qualified individuals. The fact remains that we have a very large number of unemployed people at this time with under-employment running at a rate of approximately 15%.

---

[48] The Dodd-Frank bill came into being in reaction to the housing financial disaster. "We've got to control those that caused the problem." The problem is, there is no general agreement on the detailed causes of the housing disaster that drove us into recession, but the restrictions of Dodd-Frank aren't designed help us recover. They are designed to try to prevent a future financial problem. Nice to have that protection, but we've got an urgent employment problem.

Besides providing excellent education in the future, we need to be concerned with the status of those who are currently unemployed. I've suggested that an incentive system should be put into place, that gives the unemployed a modest income while they're being trained and give employers tax credit for taking on these individuals and providing the necessary training.

- ❏ <u>Tax break for corporations</u>. In a free market capitalist system most companies and individuals are selling their products and services in a very competitive marketplace. This puts pressure on prices and has the effect of keeping profits down. This fact drives many companies to outsource their manufacturing in order to lower their costs of goods, and thus improve their profitability.

The profitability of the entity is important because its growth rate is dependent upon its return on equity. Since we want to expand the economy it makes sense to not overdo taxation, which depletes profitability in any given competitive situation. With the U.S. paying one of the highest corporate tax rates in the world, we should look at lowering corporate tax rates in order to enable companies to better fund their growth. To those that are concerned about collection of corporate taxes, I suggest that the correct solution involves streamlining the tax code, rather than leaving the top tax rate at 35%.

The Living Wage Benefit

At the beginning of this book I set out the two goals of reducing unemployment and reducing poverty in our country. Both goals are important in light of the severe underemployment situation that we now face. The Living Wage Benefit is key to both economic recovery and the reduction of poverty.[49]

❑ <u>Creates additional markets.</u>   The Living Wage, implemented as a Benefit, not a requirement, expands the market for goods and services in the U.S. and is thus an important aspect of economic recovery.

❑ <u>As a Benefit</u>. We, as a country, need to work towards implementation of a Living Wage Benefit, to be granted by companies just like any other benefit employed in a competitive job market.

❑ <u>Public awareness as a motivator.</u> Adherence to the Living Wage Benefit can become a positive public relations factor for companies, a positive competitive factor to attract customers, if you will.

❑ <u>Retain free market capitalism.</u>   In the process of promoting the Living Wage Benefit, we need to ensure that it does not become a constraining require-ment on U.S. companies.   Doing so would have disastrous consequences in terms of killing entry level and part-time jobs that are critical to young people's development.

---

[49] In 1914 Henry Ford introduced a $5.00 per day minimum wage strategy in his factories, at a time when the average autoworker wage was $2.34 for a 9 hour shift. Many have said that this was his way of creating a middle class that could buy his cars. He was quoted as saying it was one of his best cost cutting moves ever made, reducing turnover and training costs. Regardless of the motivation, his action had the consequence of putting purchasing power into the hands of the employees.

Minimum Wages

A Federal minimum wage rule is in place and most states have their own rates. The minimum wage rates, if raised to higher levels, will be a deterrent to hiring. They should not be used as a means of correcting unemployment problems.

Health Care Costs

Health care costs, and thus health insurance costs have risen significantly over the years. At the current time, most health care insurance is provided by employers – the Affordable Care Act may change that. Regardless, healthcare costs represent an expense to companies that is paid for by increasing prices of goods and services. In a competitive world, control of these costs is therefore important. There are steps that can be taken to control these costs.

- ❑ <u>Liability limits.</u> Most agree that lawsuits over health care are causing significant increases in health care costs. Limiting the liability will help control costs, without reducing benefits to the ordinary person.

- ❑ <u>Incentives.</u> Medicare and other insurance programs allow one to obtain health care services at no cost to the individual for each instance. An incentive system should be put into place that puts the insured in the position of judging the need for care. The free market works best when consumers have a stake in the process.

Keeping Jobs at Home

The shift to foreign outsourcing for our manufacturing needs has been dramatic. Driven by the free market, this loss of jobs is a major part of the current unemployment problem. There are steps than can be taken to reverse this trend and bring the jobs back to the U.S.

- ❑ <u>Tax law incentives.</u> The federal tax law can be modified to provide incentives for companies to execute their manufacturing in the U.S. Incentives built around the maximum corporate tax rate, which is already the highest in the world, are a good start at encouraging manufacturing at home.

- ❑ <u>Elimination of "Dumping."</u> The federal government can step in to help by being aggressive in pursuit of foreign companies that are dumping (selling at below cost) products into the U.S. market.

- ❑ <u>Made in the U.S.A.</u> An emphasis on a Made in the U.S.A. campaign can help influence manufacturers to bring jobs back home. We need to take some personal responsibility here and let companies know that we want to see quality products Made in the U.S.A.

Imports and Free Trade

We can be a good participant in the new global economy by continuing to allow imports (based on market demand) of products made outside the U.S. Our criteria for importing need to include protection from dumping. Free trade agreements with other countries can provide healthy import/export activities.

Environmental Regulations

Some current and many proposed environmental regulations have a significant effect on stifling the economy, thus preventing job growth.

- ❏ <u>Balance.</u> We need, at this time, to strike a better balance between environmental protection needs and the needs of man. The impact of regulations on our ability to develop our society needs to be a key part of environmental policy decisions.

- ❏ <u>Efficient legal process.</u> We need to ensure that the legal processes for environmental review are followed. Currently, the politically motivated (at times a minority) can extend the review process for years through legal challenges. We need government bodies to follow the law and expedite the review process. Fast tracking might be used where appropriate.

- ❏ <u>Set priorities.</u> We need to set our priorities when it comes to environmental protection and man-made global warming. We have two choices.

  - ✓ Zero defect environment? We can continue our drive for a zero defect environment, setting policies and regulations wherein the cost to employment is of little or no concern. "Let the economy sort itself out – the environment is more important."

  - ✓ Or, we can give the priority to getting our economic house in order first. Development of the economy with the resulting achievement of more rational unemployment rates can provide a much better base from which to further consider environmental improvements.

The latter approach has the advantage of developing the economy to help correct underemployment and help reduce deficit spending (in itself a very serious problem). As with your own personal finances, being fiscally responsible will prevent later financial disaster.

Energy

Analysis of our balance of foreign trade problem shows that a good part of the imports we make are for oil. Currently we import a little less than half of our needs. There are steps that we can be taking that can reduce our dependence on foreign oil. Such action will help stem the flow of cash from this country, and has the potential to provide for better employment opportunities in a number of ways.

- ❏ Offshore development. We can and should provide efficient review for the granting of new development licenses for the Gulf oil fields. The BP disaster was a reminder that accidents can and will happen. There is no way we can have a zero defect society, and lengthy delays in granting permits will not produce zero defects.

- ❏ Northern Slope oil development. We have most of the transportation needs in place and have performed endless environmental reviews for further development of the Northern Alaskan oil fields. We should be allowing this development to move forward, in the interest of gaining independence from foreign oil.

- ❏ Nuclear power plants. We also have to recognize that we do not have an infinite supply of oil and natural gas. Eventually, and very likely a long distance in the future, we need to have developed alternate sources of energy. Towards that end, nuclear power still represents an attractive alternative source, provided we can develop intrinsically safer power plant designs and solve spent fuel disposal problems. We should therefore have an active development program in place, probably supported, at least in part, by the federal government. We should view with caution some of the current solutions to renewable energy and hydrocarbon free emissions.

❑ <u>The auto industry.</u> The auto industry in the U.S. is in the recovery mode, after bankruptcies by GM and Chrysler. The auto manufacturers are a major source of employment for the country. The government needs to be practical in setting regulations, such as required average fuel mileage. The costs of meeting unrealistic regulations can again force these companies into financial stress.

In striving to achieve environmental goals, especially with regard to hydrocarbon emissions, we need to have practical regulations. Along with that, we need to have practical measurements of performance, including consideration of the source of energy used in charging batteries.

❑ <u>Food as an energy source.</u> In the quest for foreign oil independence and establishment of renewable energy sources, the government has encouraged, by setting up subsidies, the use of corn to create ethanol. While this might seem like a laudable cause, it has the disastrous effect of raising corn and other food prices, which can hit the poor especially hard. We, as a nation, need to shift away from this ill-conceived program, launched in the interest of achieving renewable sources of energy. There are better solutions.

❑   Transportable sources of energy.   Since foreign oil payments constitute such a large portion of our balance of trade problem and we are striving hard to reduce hydrocarbon emissions, we as a country should focus on practical solutions to achieving hydrocarbon-free transportable sources of energy. One solution that is being tried utilizes the hydrogen fuel cell. This technology, when coupled with nuclear power plant generated electricity to generate the hydrogen, achieves a true hydrocarbon free solution to powering the automobile. We should be pushing development of this technology.

There have been other attempts to achieve transportable sources of energy for the automobile, including battery packs charged from non-polluting sources of electricity, gyroscopically powered drives and solar powered autos. All have serious range limitations.

Economic Stability

A key factor in the willingness of companies to invest in growth opportunities is the stability of the economy. That is to say, we need stable policies, regulations, tax rates and incentives if we are to see companies be willing to make the necessary investments. Short-term incentives, for example, do not help much in terms of long term planning.

Corporate and personal income tax rates should be set for a reasonably long period of time (years, not months) so that intelligent planning can take place. If an overhaul of the tax system is desired, it should be done without the pressure of impending deadlines that introduce uncertainty into the economy.

Development of the Infrastructure

In many cases, development of the infrastructure may be necessary to support development. This type of work, best financed through the government, but possibly with toll support, should be done on a long term planning basis,[50] to balance new projects with the need for repair/replacement projects.

Restructure Public Employee Benefits

The economic downturn has revealed, in many instances, the problems created by exorbitant benefit packages granted some public employees. These benefit packages can have the effect of draining taxpayer dollars from funding ongoing operations. Restructuring these packages will create employment opportunities with government agencies.

---

[50] At present economists in the U.S. are extremely concerned with the size of the nation's debt and the continuing annual deficits. With such worries, it is unlikely that massive infrastructure stimulus programs should or will be approved by Congress. Again, focusing on revitalization of the economy in the private sector will provide more revenues for the government, thus allowing for better control of the debt and eventually more infrastructure work.

It is reasonable to work towards leveling the playing field. If the government sets up one set of rules for retirees (such as 401 (k)'s, would not it be reasonable for government employees to work under the same terms and conditions? The goal should not be to arbitrarily dismantle current benefits, but to modify to create more reasonable benefit packages.

Financing for Housing Bubble Victims

With the large number of housing foreclosures that have taken place in the last 6 years, a significant number of individuals/families will be out of the housing market for a number of years. The problem is their credit rating. While some undoubtedly gamed the system, many folks were lulled into the myth that home prices would be forever ascending. These forks are usually employed and would represent qualified buyers in a normal housing market.

Since the housing market is driven by demand, the sooner these folks can get back into the market, the better for new construction, and thus new jobs.

It would seem logical to set up a means for financing such individuals, perhaps through lease option buy programs. The result would be a benefit for the individuals and a benefit for the country.

Full Transparency Monitoring

Throughout this book I have made suggestions that should help the country solve some of its underemployment problems. Often the key to fixing problems is to first thoroughly understand them. Without a good understanding, we can head off in the wrong direction. This suggests that full transparency monitoring of parameters on the economy will go a long ways towards educating government officials and employees on the needs and progress made in the employment area.

The need is particularly true in the government reporting of employment in the U.S. Classical unemployment rates that have been reported can mask the true nature of the problem. The public, and legislators have to have a common understanding of these measures of success or failure. While it may be temping to emphasize favorable numbers over the unfavorable for whatever reasons, it makes a lot of sense to just lay the numbers out and then work to achieve the employment goals.

Living Wage Calculations

Throughout this book I have pushed for the payment of the Living Wage Benefit. For such a program to work, we need determination of Living Wage levels in the various parts of the country. A means for determination needs to be set up. The studies should use common methods to arrive at Living Wage levels that can be utilized by employers in determining their adherence to such a program.

The Voter Responsibility

Finally, I urge you, as a voter, to try to sort out the position of the various candidates on the issues that have been discussed. There is an urgent need for elected officials to also spend the time to best understand the issues we face, and the corrective approaches that make sense.

With 31 million people unemployed and 46 million living below the poverty line, "Houston, we've got a problem."

Acknowledgements

I wish to acknowledge my wife Bonnie and the rest of my family for their support of my various endeavors in life. I also wish to acknowledge Dr. Godfrey Mungal, Dean of the School of Engineering at Santa Clara University for giving me the opportunity to travel to Nicaragua in 2011, thus re-opening my eyes to the plight of impoverished societies.

About the Author

Mr. Cantoni is a retired high technology executive with an extensive background of work in many different fields, including 35 years in medical instrumentation. He has been described as a serial entrepreneur. He was born in Napa, California and spent his early years on a ranch in Napa County. While not born into poverty, he was quite familiar with the wearing of hand-me-down clothes.

Mr. Cantoni is a graduate of Santa Clara University, earning a Bachelor of Science degree in Electrical Engineering, and Stanford University, earning a Master of Science degree in Electrical Engineering. He benefited from family financial support in the process of obtaining his college degrees.

Since this book has been about the creation of jobs in the U.S. it might be appropriate to include a discussion of his work history; in essence, a "full disclosure" statement, in case you are wondering what gave him the background to write this book. The list is lengthy, but illustrates the broad and in-depth experiences he has had, including that as founder or co-founder and President and CEO of three high tech startup companies.

To quote Mr. Cantoni, "I was born and raised on a ranch in Napa, California and began my first work experiences at the age of eight. The ranch was planted in prunes and grapes and provided summer work for my brother and I. Our family moved to the Santa Clara Valley (now Silicon Valley) in 1946. Following is a summary of my work experience. (The brackets {} indicate the company financial structure.).

- At age 15 I started working summers for a cooperative dryer (the world's largest at that time) in Campbell, California, initially as an APT (all purpose tool). At age 16 I started driving forklift and by age 18 I was promoted to chief maintenance supervisor for the dryer plant. From that work experience I figured out that I could learn a skill and enjoy employing that skill in my job. I came away from the dryer employment experience having worked as a mechanic, electrician, welder, and all around equipment construction and repair person. {Private Cooperative}

- At age 21. I worked for one summer as a sheet metal apprentice for a company building bean harvesters. Took part in my first and only union election. {Private Company}

- I graduated with a BSEE from Santa Clara University in 1957 and a MSEE from Stanford University in 1958.

- From 1958 through 1960 I served in the U.S. Army Signal Corps and was honorably discharged with the rank of 1st Lieutenant. The Army provided my first management experience, assigning me as Operations Officer for a signal intelligence-gathering unit, based at Ft. Monmouth, New Jersey.

- In 1960 I began my career in Silicon Valley as a design engineer. {Division of a large public corporation}
- In 1961 I became a founding partner of a chicken feed business in Alberta, Canada that was operated by one of the partners. Valuable experience in learning about partnerships, but not the financial success envisioned. The partnership was funded by the six founding partners and bank loans. {Small partnership}
- In 1964 I joined a startup in Palo Alto, CA founded by William J. Perry (later Secretary of Defense for President Bill Clinton), Clarence S. Jones (my mentor) and others. The company was in the electronic defense business and provided an entry for me into senior management. It was funded at startup by its employees and eventually went public. {Startup corporation that went public}
- In 1970, I co-founded a medical imaging company, established to carry electronic defense ideas into the nuclear medicine market. I became president of the company in 1976 and took the company public in 1979. Grew the company to $70 Million in revenues by 1984, employing approximately 1,200 people. The company designed, developed and sold/serviced medical products on a worldwide basis. The company was funded initially by the co-founders, and later brought in modest venture capital investment before going public in 1979. The company was eventually sold to a major medical imaging company. {Startup corporation that we took public, eventually merged out}
- In 1982, invested in Limited Partnerships that were the start-up vehicles for Adobe Systems and Genentech. {Investment Limited Partnerships}

- Co-founded another medical imaging company in 1985. The company designed, developed and sold specialized image processing systems for medical and other applications. This startup was funded initially by the founders, then by serious venture capital. The company developed sound products, but was not successful in the marketplace. {Private corporation}

- Formed a Sub-chapter-S company in 1988, selling and eventually developing hardware and software systems for cardiac catheterization labs. Sold the company in 1994 to a division of a large public company. Retired in 1998. {Private Sub-chapter S Corporation, merged out}

- In 2004, re-entered the workplace as President and CEO of another medical imaging company. Finally retired in 2005. {Small private corporation, Venture Capital financed}

Along the way, I served as a board member of an industry association (NEMA Medical Imaging Division), a non-profit hospital (Alexian Brothers of San Jose, CA), the Board of Regents at Santa Clara University, the Santa Clara University School of Engineering Industry Advisory Board, a public Silicon Valley high tech company, a public medical imaging company, a California Special District providing utility services to a small community, and as a member of the Board of Directors of various private companies."